VEBLEN IN PLAIN ENGLISH

A Complete Introduction to Thorstein Veblen's Economics

Ken McCormick

CAMBRIA
PRESS

YOUNGSTOWN, NEW YORK

This book has been registered with the Library of Congress.
McCormick, Ken
      Veblen in Plain English / Ken McCormick
      p. cm.
      Includes bibliographical references
      ISBN 0-977-3567-6-0

For Danita

Contents

FOREWORD

Although scholars disagree about the significance of his work, interest in Thorstein Veblen (1857-1929) has not decreased. Born in 1857 in Wisconsin, Veblen was the fourth child of Norwegian immigrant farmers who raised a large family, most of whom received higher education. The Veblen children went to Carleton College in Northfield, Minnesota; there Thorstein obtained his training in economics and philosophy under the tutelage of John Bates Clark, who later became a prominent neoclassical economist. After receiving his bachelor's degree at Carleton, Veblen taught for a year and then enrolled at Johns Hopkins for graduate study. After a short stay, he transferred to Yale, where he obtained his Ph.D. in philosophy in 1884, while studying under such noted academicians as Noah Porter and William Graham Sumner.

Veblen was then idle for seven years, most of which was spent on the farms of relatives or in-laws in the Midwest. His agnosticism made him unemployable in schools with religious affiliations, and he had not yet established a reputation in economics. Finally, in 1891 he obtained a graduate position at Cornell University, where he once again became a doctoral student. The economist James Laurence Laughlin was impressed by him, and in 1892, when Laughlin moved to the newly founded University of Chicago, he took Veblen with him. Veblen soon became editor of the *Journal of Political Economy* and began publishing in the field of economics. In 1899 his most famous book, *The Theory of the Leisure Class*, appeared and achieved a notoriety all its own. But Veblen's personal idiosyncrasies and his failure to properly "advertise" the university offended the administration at Chicago, and he was forced to move. His next job was at Stanford where, in a few short years, he encountered similar difficulties. He was compelled to move again, this time to the University of Missouri.

World War I found Veblen briefly in Washington as an employee of the U.S. Food Administration. After the war, he served for a short time as one of the editors of the Dial, a journal of literary and political opinion, and as a member of the faculty of the recently founded New School for Social Research in New York City. By then, even though his reputation as a scholar and publicist was at its peak, his academic career was at an end. Veblen retired and moved to California, near Stanford, where he died in August 1929, shortly before the onset of the Depression.

The economist Wesley C. Mitchell, who as student, colleague and friend of Veblen knew him as well and as long as anyone outside his family and possessed an intimate familiarity with his writings, commented in 1934 that "Thorstein Veblen is the most fascinating and the most enigmatic social thinker of our times. He explains others to themselves as the curious products of age-long processes of social change; but behind the glittering analysis that has shocked thousands into consciousness of their artificialities, he stays a mysterious figure, coming from a dim half-alien world to show the wonder of what we cannot see because it is so commonplace."[1] Such was the man whose economics are here interpreted.

Professor Ken McCormick's study of Veblen's economics is intended for the student and the non-specialist. Veblen's significant ideas about economists, economics and the economy are presented so as to illuminate his distinctions between business and industry, that is, making money versus making socially useful goods. McCormick also focuses on emulatory versus instrumental consumption or the use of status enhancing goods as opposed to commodities that increase our biological and adaptive well being. And to what ends should the economy be geared? To what Veblen calls the "generic ends of life" — the expansion of "altruism" or other-regardingness, "idle curiosity" or critical intelligence, and proficiency of "workmanship" — taking pains with work and pride arising out of craftsmanship as both a socially and self-fulfilling process.

He emphasized the social nature of wealth production as opposed to private claims on the social product, equalitarian distribution instead of elitist demands for privileged access to goods and services; all of the above are an integral part of what Veblen hoped would be a movement in the direction of an "industrial republic." Veblen also supported avoidance of waste through full utilization of the industrial plant and labor force. This was to be accompanied by a decline in conspicuous display, invidious dissipation of resources in religious superstition, sports and gambling, competitive rivalry and honorific prowess. As should now be evident, Veblen's jargon suggests the need to keep a dictionary close at hand, but the student and non-specialist can soon master enough of his vocabulary to grasp the main thrust of his remarks.

What Veblen attacks as the "ceremonial" appears throughout the social order in the form of pockets of irrationality and inequity. McCormick skillfully interprets the ceremonial in the society in which we now live as he brings to life the vestiges and residues, some might say the preponderance of the ceremonial which he and Veblen would replace with a more rational and just existence. Underlying the latter are the forces of progressive change which are found in the ethos and practice of science, the secularism and egalitarianism secured by the advance of technology as well as humanistic ends; in short, the upsurge of the generic ends of life, impersonally considered.

Yet lurking in the shadows are the persistence of atavistic continuities and imbecile institutions whose regressive resurgence in the form of war, exploitation, waste and superstition still threaten humankind. Neither Veblen nor McCormick are Pollyannas who believe we have reached the land of milk and honey where we can live together peaceably under conditions of voluntary simplicity and economic abundance. But such a tranquil order has now appeared on the historical scene and political agenda as a distinct possibility whose ultimate realization is worth striving for.

Rick Tilman

Adjunct Professor of History

Northern Arizona University

Footnotes
[1] Wesley Mitchell to B. W. Huebsch, July 14, 1934, Joseph Dorfman Collection, Butler Library, Columbia University, New York City.

PREFACE

My objective in writing this book is modest: to write a concise introduction to Thorstein Veblen's economics that is easily accessible to non-specialists and students. I have had an abiding interest in Thorstein Veblen's economics for most of my professional life. Occasionally colleagues and students have asked me if there is a book they could read to learn more about Veblen's economics. The first time I heard the question I assumed that the answer must be yes. The literature on Veblen is vast. Surely there was something I could refer others to that would serve as a reliable and readable introduction to his major economic arguments.

But the truth is that precious little of the Veblen literature is written for the non-specialist. Moreover, much of what has been written focuses on matters other than his economics. The problem has been recognized for some time. In 1954 A. W. Coats complained that while much had been written about Veblen's work, very little of it had to do with his economics [Coats, 1954, 529]. In 1977 Donald Walker repeated the complaint. He wrote that most of the articles and books on Veblen

> rather than concentrating on his economic doc-
> trines...have been concerned in a diffuse and epi-
> sodic way with his ideas in a variety of disciplines, or
> have reviewed his philosophical and methodological
> ideas, or have attempted to deal with his background,
> to place him in the context of American culture, and
> to discuss his psychological peculiarities. Many
> articles have been written on Veblen's sociological
> ideas...[Walker, 1977, 213].

Walker attempted to fill the void with an article on Veblen's economic system. While his article has its virtues, it fails to present the
full power and sweep of Veblen's ideas. In Walker's defense, it is
impossible to do so in a single article.

A recent book by Adil Mouhammed, An Introduction to Thorstein
Veblen's Economic Theory [2003], is not for the uninitiated. It requires significant knowledge of the history of economic thought and
lays heavy stress on methodology. In addition, the book has a strong
Marxian flavor that, in my view, is not appropriate for Veblen.

One could, of course, refer people to Veblen's own writing. But
as anyone who has ever read Veblen knows, reading Veblen is not
for the faint of heart. Veblen does provide the occasional sparkling
phrase, and his satire is legendary. For the connoisseur, Veblen's
style can sometimes even be a thing of joy. But that cannot mask
the fact that his prose is very hard to read and his ideas are not conveniently organized. For most readers, Veblen is simply too much
work. As one sympathetic observer put it,

> The chief reason why Veblen has not been more
> widely read is his style, which is so marked with tor-
> tuous clauses and involuted phrases that one some-

times wonders whether Veblen did not do all in his
power to hide his ideas from those who might utilize
them [Herskovits, 1936, 352].

The end result is that one cannot recommend that someone with a
little curiosity about Veblen go read Veblen. All but the most determined readers will give up. I have seen it happen many times.

My goal is to write a book that meets three criteria. The first is
that it is short. My intention is to write an inviting introduction, not
an exhaustive treatise. The second is that it should be accessible to
non-specialists and students. That means that the book should be
easy to read and should not assume too much about the reader's
background. The third is to present accurately Veblen's ideas about
economics.

My work is informed by the light shed on Veblen by many previous writers, to whom I owe a very large debt of gratitude. I am
conscious, however, of Thomas Sowell's admonition that Veblen's
interpreters "do not always sharply distinguish the words of the
master from the traditions of the followers" [Sowell, 1967, 177]. In
some cases, the divergence has become quite sharp. My intention is
to stick as closely as possible to Veblen's original ideas. Of course,
my interpretation of Veblen is just that; others may have different
interpretations.

Because of how Veblen worked, it will be necessary to wander
into areas not universally viewed as economics. Veblen himself
showed little enthusiasm for disciplinary boundaries. But my intent
is to stay focused, as far as possible, on his work as it pertains to
economic ideas. As suggested above, the literature on other aspects
of Veblen is already extensive and rich.

ACKNOWLEDGEMENTS

Many people have helped me on this project, but there are some who deserve special recognition. Rick Tilman, William Waller and Bryce Kanago graciously volunteered to read earlier versions of the manuscript. Their comments greatly improved the final result. Of course, any remaining errors are my responsibility. Tom Kompas and Dudley Luckett introduced me to Veblen many years ago. Obviously, they made a lasting impression. The members of the economics department at the University of Northern Iowa have been a constant source of support and encouragement. They are good economists and even better people. I view them as my extended family. Roy Adams, David Hakes and Keith Heimforth have had a long-term impact on my development as an economist. Cambria Press made the publishing process much smoother and faster than I ever imagined. The Graduate College of the University of Northern Iowa provided financial support for a semester. And without the love and support of my wife Danita, nothing would be possible.

INTRODUCTION

Thorstein Veblen (1857-1929) is best remembered as an exception-
ally skilled critic. C. Wright Mills called him "the best critic of America that America has produced" [Mills, 1953, vi]. Joseph Spengler
likened him to a one-man "Ministry of Disturbance" [1972, 861].
Rick Tilman echoed these sentiments decades later when he wrote
that Veblen "was arguably the most original and penetrating economist and social critic that the United States has produced" [Tilman,
1992, ix]. As it stands, Veblen's reputation rests on his formidable
assault on conventional thinking, as well as on his ability to coin a
few memorable phrases such as "conspicuous consumption."

But to conceive of Veblen as only a critic is a mistake. As E. K.
Hunt noted, Veblen was also "probably the most significant, original
and profound social theorist in American history" [Hunt, 1979, 300].
Veblen did not engage in criticism just for the sake of criticism;
his purpose was to explain why a new approach to economics was
needed. Veblen's ultimate objective was to re-invent the discipline
of economics.

Ever since Adam Smith, economics has modeled itself on the physical sciences, especially Newtonian mechanics. Smith was so impressed with Newton's system that he called it "the greatest discovery that was ever made by man" [Smith, 1795, 105]. Over one hundred years later, Vilfredo Pareto, one of Veblen's contemporaries, was still talking about economics in terms of Newtonian mechanics. Pareto wrote that "the problem of pure economics bears a striking likeness to that of rational mechanics" [Pareto, 1897, 490].

By modeling itself on Newtonian mechanics, economics was led down the path to equilibrium analysis. As every student of economics knows, equilibrium analysis is central to mainstream economics. Even growth theory, which would seem to be about anything but equilibrium, is often discussed in terms of a steady-state, which "represents the long-run equilibrium of the economy" [Mankiw, 2003, 186]. There are even jokes about it: "Old economists never die; they just lose their equilibrium." Evidently for an economist, losing one's equilibrium is the end of the road.

For some purposes, equilibrium analysis is useful. But to Veblen, the really important questions in economics were self-evidently not about equilibria. The most striking feature of a market capitalist economy is its rapid pace of change. All other known economic systems seem sluggish in comparison. Why is it that economists spend so much time on static equilibrium analysis when the most obvious feature of the economy is constant upheaval and change? As Veblen put it, "The question now before the body of economists is not how things stabilise themselves in a 'static state,' but how they endlessly grow and change" [1934, 8].

Veblen argued that economics should look to Darwin, not Newton, for its inspiration. Economic growth and development is an evolutionary process. Static analysis has its uses, but questions such as how real economies develop over time require an approach that focuses on the process of change. To this end, Veblen envisioned an "evolutionary" approach to economics. As he saw it,

> an evolutionary economics must be the theory of a process of cultural growth as determined by the economic interest, a theory of a cumulative sequence of economic institutions stated in terms of the process itself [Veblen, 1919, 77].

Economics must seek to explain change, which is the most obvious feature of a modern economy.

The most pressing question in economics is how to transform impoverished nations into prosperous ones. As Nobel laureate Robert Lucas put it, once one begins to think about how to make poor countries rich, "it is hard to think about anything else" [1988, 5]. To find the solution, one must recognize that the necessary changes are not just quantitative but also qualitative. Economic development is not primarily about producing more widgets; it is about transforming the entire society in a myriad of different ways. The modern American economy is not just a larger replica of the American economy of one hundred years ago. It is dramatically different in most every aspect of economic life. Not only are the goods and services different, but so are the perspectives and habits of thought of the population. In addition, the economic changes and the cultural changes that have occurred are intimately related. They must be examined together as part of one integral process. Economics must develop an analytical structure capable of doing so. Anything less falls short of what is required for the task at hand.

Of course, to argue that economics should be an evolutionary discipline is not the same as actually creating an evolutionary economics. It must be clear from the outset that Veblen did not create a full-blown, systematic evolutionary economics. There is not even a consensus on the degree to which he made clear exactly what he envisioned. At one extreme is Sowell, who argues that Veblen gave only "sparse and sketchy" [1967, 178] hints as to what an evolutionary economics would look like. At the other extreme is Hodgson, who argues that he left us "with plentiful hints and insights, many of which are brilliant, several contradictory ... his significance for evolutionary economics in particular, and economics in general, remains underestimated to this day" [1992, 327].

The underlying assumption of this book is that Hodgson was closer to the truth. Veblen left us with enough of a vision to make it worth our while to examine his ideas in detail. We should not expect to find answers to all our questions, but we will find a vibrant approach to economics that has been largely ignored by the bulk of the economics profession. A revival of interest in Veblen's project is worthwhile. Modern economics has had some successes, but, just as Veblen complained over a century ago, it is incapable of explaining the process of change. Veblen was not able to reach his own ambitious goal. But that does not mean that it is not worth pursuing. It is hoped that this work might even inspire a few people to meet his challenge to create a whole new way to do economics.[1]

An essential element in Veblen's vision is that the evolution of an economy is non-teleological. That means that the system is not headed to any pre-ordained end. Darwinian evolution is open-ended, and the direction of change cannot be foretold. There is no pre-determined ending point such as the long-run equilibrium of neoclassical[2] economics or the Communism of Marxism. There is not even an inescapable drift toward improvement. A priori, there is only change. Veblen wrote that

> The evolutionary point of view ... leaves no place for a formulation of natural laws in terms of definitive normality, whether in economics or in any other branch of inquiry. Neither does it leave room for that other question of normality, What should be the end of the developmental process under discussion? [1919,76].

Predicting the future is impossible. No human can know the final outcome of an evolutionary process.

A second important feature of Veblen's vision is that the evolutionary idea was to him more than just a metaphor. Veblen read Darwin quite carefully [Edgell, 2001]. Darwin's ideas were of central importance to Veblen. Veblen was well-versed in the evolutionary biology of his time, which is something that few economists could say today. Edgell goes so far as to say that "the Darwinian influence on Veblen is even more profound than has previously been judged to be the case" [2001, 86-7].

It seemed natural to Veblen to apply evolutionary thinking to the economy, where one observes the same continuous, gradual, cumulative change as in the biological world. To that end, he sought to identify the elements in the economic sphere that are analogous to the elements necessary for evolution in the biological sphere. For example, what is it in the economy that is subject to natural selection? How are characteristics passed on from generation to generation? What are the sources of variation, without which there can be no natural selection? How does the struggle for survival play out?

Before proceeding to Veblen's answers to these questions, it is worth pausing briefly to consider Veblen's political leanings. There are elements of anarchism, socialism and technocratic elitism in his writing.[3] Those "isms" fundamentally contradict each other in important ways, so it is obvious that one cannot attach a convenient label to Veblen. The reader should jettison conventional notions of political left and right.

There is no doubt that Veblen would have preferred a more rational system than the one he saw. Very few writers can match Veblen's ability to make capitalist institutions look ridiculous. But he never attached himself closely to any political movement, or even wrote very much about politics. He was much more interested in analysis than political agitation. Part of the reason may be his method of analysis. Social engineering without a deep understanding of the evolutionary process is perilous. Tinkering with a society without such an understanding is like tinkering with a person's genes without a full understanding of what they are, how they work and how they are related.

Another reason Veblen did not embrace political movements might be that he was not optimistic about our ability to effect change. As will be discussed in more detail later, our habits of thought are deeply ingrained. We resist change, especially because we "know" that the current set of institutions is good and right. They may need a little adjusting, but fundamental change is out of the question. In a prescient passage written on the eve of World War I, Veblen famously wrote that

> ... history records more frequent and more spectacular instances of the triumph of imbecile institutions over life and culture than of peoples who have by force of instinctive insight saved themselves alive out of a desperately precarious institutional situation, such, for instance, as now faces the peoples of Christendom [1914, 19].

Only the process of evolution can effect fundamental change. As Edgell remarked, for Veblen "the most recent era is more susceptible to 'natural decay' than social engineering of an ameliorative or radical kind" [Edgell, 2001, 98].

It is also worth noting that despite Veblen's devastating attacks on the business system, he did not subscribe to the simplistic idea that capitalism's institutions were designed to benefit the rich at the expense of the poor. The point is important enough to quote Veblen at length:

> The modern industrial system is based on the institution of private property under free competition, and it cannot be claimed that these institutions have heretofore worked to the detriment of the material interests of the average member of society ... the system of industrial competition, based on private property, has brought about, or at least has co-existed with, the most rapid advance in average wealth and industrial efficiency that the world has ever seen. Especially can it fairly be claimed that the result of the last few decades of our industrial development has been to increase greatly the creature comforts of the average

> human being. And, decidedly, the result has been an
> amelioration of the lot of the less favored in a rela-
> tively greater degree than that of those economically
> more fortunate. The claim that the system of com-
> petition has proved itself an engine for making the
> rich richer and the poor poorer has the fascination of
> epigram; but if its meaning is that the lot of the aver-
> age, of the masses of humanity in civilised life, is
> worse today, as measured in the means of livelihood,
> than it was twenty, or fifty, or a hundred years ago,
> then it is farcical [1919, 391].

Capitalism has without a doubt improved the material standard of living of the average person. Its problems and deficiencies lie elsewhere.

The beginning of the twenty-first century finds us with no serious alternatives to capitalism. Various political factions agitate for change of greater or lesser magnitude. But only true ideologues, blind to history, really believe that a fundamentally different system would necessarily be an improvement, or that it could be brought about without enormous bloodshed. That makes Veblen's approach and analysis all the more valuable. He made no attempt to construct castles in the air to which the march of history is inevitably taking us. There is only the hard business of looking at human society as it is and trying to make sense of it. As Diggins put it, "capitalism is something we must learn to live with [and that] makes Veblen's critical perspectives more pertinent than ever" [1999, xxix]. Veblen's approach offers an antidote to the tired ideologies espoused by the demagogues who dominate public discourse.

PART I
INSTINCTS
AND INSTITUTIONS

Ultimately, economics is about human behavior. That is why every system of economic analysis must include a description of how people behave. Not surprisingly, different schools of thought present very different views. Before we look at Veblen's ideas on the subject, it will be instructive to examine the views of the two major schools of thought that existed at the time Veblen was writing. As we shall see, the contrast with Veblen is stark.

Neoclassical economists had an extraordinarily simple view of human nature, which they believed to be the same at all times and places. People, because they are people, were all assumed to be utility maximizers. That means that all behavior can be explained as rational attempts either to obtain pleasure or to avoid pain. Economists of the time wrote about people as hedonistic utility maximizers in stark terms. Edgeworth, for example, spoke of humans as "pleasure machines" [Edgeworth, 1881, 15]. People calculated the likely pleasures and pains associated with various actions, and then chose the ones that gave them the most pleasure. To be fair, it should be noted that defenders of this hedonistic approach argued that "pleasure" included mental and spiritual pleasure as well as physical pleasure [Mill, 1961, 195].

The idea that people only react to pleasure and pain struck Veblen as absurd. The neoclassical approach presents people as passive, re-active agents. Veblen believed that a person "is not simply a bundle of desires that are to be saturated ... but rather a coherent structure of propensities and habits which seek realization and expression in unfolding activities" [1919, 74]. If there were no pleasure to be had or pain to be avoided, would we really sit still and do nothing at all? Moreover, do people really make the calculations required to maximize utility? Veblen satirized the hedonistic view of human nature in a famous passage that illustrates both his biting wit and the difficulty of reading his prose:

> The psychological and anthropological preconceptions of the economists have been those which were accepted by the psychological and social sciences some generations ago. The hedonistic conception of man is that of a lightning calculator of pleasures and pains, who oscillates like a homogeneous globule of desire of happiness under the impulse of stimuli that shift him about the area, but leave him intact. He has neither antecedent nor consequent. He is an isolated, definitive human datum, in stable equilibrium except for the buffets of the impinging forces that displace him in one direction or another. Self-imposed in elemental space, he spins symmetrically about his own spiritual axis until the parallelogram of forces bears

down upon him, whereupon he follows the line of the resultant. When the force of the impact is spent, he comes to rest, a self-contained globule of desire as before. Spiritually, the hedonistic man is not a prime mover. He is not the seat of a process of living, except in the sense that he is subject to a series of permutations enforced upon him by circumstances external and alien to him [Veblen, 1919, 73-4].

Partly because of Veblen's satire, modern neoclassical economists no longer openly embrace Edgeworth's shocking view of human nature. Modern neoclassical economists continue to assume that people are utility maximizers, but they claim that it is only a modeling device. In other words, they do not openly say that people really are pleasure machines. The assumption is made because, in their view, models based on the assumption of utility maximization predict well. The approach is defended in Milton Friedman's famous article, "The Methodology of Positive Economics" [1953]. Friedman argues that a model's ability to predict is the only thing that matters in judging how good the model is. In his view, the realism of the assumptions is irrelevant. It follows that one can assume whatever one wants about human behavior as long as one's model predicts well. What is left unspoken is the fact that while the approach may be useful for predicting seasonal variations in the consumption of ice cream, it is not capable of addressing more fundamental questions such as the evolution of economic institutions. For Veblen, these more fundamental questions were of primary importance.

The main alternative to neoclassical economics at the time was the economics of Karl Marx. Marx was interested in some of the same basic questions as Veblen, but took an approach different from both Veblen and the neoclassical economists. In Marx's view, one's behavior is shaped by one's circumstances. How one acts and thinks depends on one's social class. Workers think differently than owners because their experiences are so different. Ironically, the only trait common to all classes is one that would be right at home in neoclassical analysis, namely rational self-interest. Class struggle occurs as different classes fight to advance or to protect their interests. The idea of class struggle clearly presupposes that members of each class understand their interests. This means that they are capable of penetrating the veneer of society and perceiving its deeper reality.

As history progresses, both material and social conditions change. According to Marx, human behavior must inevitably change as well because external conditions determine how people think. As Marx famously put it, "It is not the consciousness of men that determines their existence, but, on the contrary, their social existence that determines their consciousness" [Marx, 1859, 4]. Unlike the neoclassical view that posits an unchanging human nature, Marx believes that human nature is a product of the environment. To put it differently, the neoclassical view is that human behavior is completely determined by nature, and Marx's view is that it is determined completely by nurture.

Veblen's view of human behavior is more complex than that of either the neoclassical economists or of Marx. In his view, both nature and nurture shape human behavior. Nature endows humans with innate behavioral tendencies that Veblen called instincts. Instincts are themselves subject to evolutionary change over long periods of time. Nurture, in the form of institutions such as learned habits of thought and social conventions, also influence our behavior. Institutions can also evolve and change over time.

Instincts are much broader than the simple pleasure seeking / pain avoidance of the neoclassical school. There are many different facets of human nature. We are complex beings, and our instincts may sometimes even contradict each other. To understand human behavior, we must begin by examining instincts and institutions.

CHAPTER 1

INSTINCTS

Veblen saw people as active agents. They have "propensities and habits which seek realisation and expression in unfolding activity" [Veblen, 1919, 74]. In other words, people have purposes which go beyond a simple pleasure-pain calculation. Even in the absence of external stimulation, people will "do something." They have innate tendencies that cause them to act.

Veblen defined instincts as "the innate and persistent propensities of human nature" [1914, 2]. They are "irreducible traits of human nature" [Ibid. 3]. Veblen was uncomfortable with the word "instinct." He said that the word "is of too imprecise a character to serve the needs of an exhaustive psychological analysis" [Ibid. 2]. Veblen used the word instinct because it comes closer than other words to capturing his meaning. It should be stressed that instincts should not be confused with what are more accurately called "tropisms." Tropisms are reflexive actions that involve no thought. An example would be pulling one's hand away from a hot stove. In contrast, instincts involve consciousness and provide the basic purposes behind human action.

The last point must be stressed. Our instincts direct our behavior in that they provide goals for our actions. We use our reason to help us figure out how to meet these goals, but reason is subservient to our instincts. As Veblen put it, "Men make thought, but the human spirit, that is to say the racial endowment of instinctive proclivities, decides what they shall take thought of, and how and to what effect" [Ibid. 6].

Broadly speaking, there are two categories of instincts. One set of instincts is group-regarding, and seeks to promote human life in general. The second set of instincts is self-regarding, and promotes the individual's interests at the expense of others. It must be understood from the beginning that these instincts are not independent and isolated from one another. They sometimes augment and sometimes contradict each other. As a moment's reflection will no doubt reveal, human beings are sometimes torn by conflicting aims.

Human instincts are the product of human evolution. It makes sense that both self-regarding and group-regarding instincts evolved. Without self-regarding instincts, individuals would not survive. But for humans, individual survival also depends on the survival of the group. We are not solitary beings. Human life is lived in groups, and the destruction of the group generally means the destruction of the individual. Recent anthropological research suggests that during the last glacial period, there was a strong selection process in favor of those willing to engage in cooperative behavior. Faced with a harsher climate and more difficult living conditions, group solidarity meant individual survival [Ambrose, 2002, 22]. As Ambrose put it, "our ancestors made the transition to cooperative networking societies early in the last ice age. Neanderthals never achieved what I call this troop-to-tribe transition" [Ambrose, 2005].

Human instincts continue to evolve, but the process is slow, perhaps too slow to matter for any period of time short of many centuries. As a result, Veblen sees instincts as more or less constant for the purpose of examining the economy. The evolution of our instincts is not the source of change in modern economies.

Prominent among our group-regarding instincts is the innate human propensity that Veblen called "parental bent." Parental bent is much more than the "quasi-tropismatic impulse" [1914, 26] to procreate. It includes not only the desire to take care of one's own children, but also a broader concern for the children of one's extended family, tribe, nation and even humanity in general. Veblen notes that it is "despicably inhuman" [Ibid. 26] for one generation willfully to make life harder for the next generation. Hence, we feel obliged not only to provide things like food, clothing and shelter for children, but we also view it necessary to provide the proper education and training so that the next generation will be able to take care of itself when the time comes.

Note that we do these things not because of rational calculation, but because it is instinctive. It is part of being human, and without it the race could not have survived. Our parental bent means that, contrary to the view of neoclassical economics, self-interest is not the only thing that motivates people. We instinctively care for others, especially the young, to at least some degree. It is not at all unusual for parents to sacrifice their own consumption for the benefit of their children. People can be induced to vote money for better schools or to donate money to orphans with the slogan, "do it for the children."

Veblen pointed out that our parental instincts run in direct opposition to the common neoclassical assumption of positive time preference. Neoclassical economists generally assume that people prefer present goods to future goods. In other words, we would rather consume now than later. As a result, people must be paid interest to induce them to save because saving requires us to delay consumption. Veblen contended that our concern for the young might induce us to save and invest simply in order to acquire more wealth for our children. As Veblen said about our parental bent,

> In the simplest and unsophisticated terms, its functional content appears to be an unselfish solicitude for the well-being of the incoming generation - a bias for the highest efficiency and fullest volume of life in the group, with a particular drift to the future; so that, under its rule, contrary to the dictum of economic theorists, future goods are preferred to present goods [Ibid. 46].

Veblen was quick to add that institutions and other instincts also affect our behavior, and will therefore affect the degree to which our parental instinct manifests. When the instinct of parenthood is strong, people will delay gratification in order to help their children. When the instinct of parenthood is weak and the self-regarding instincts are strong, children may suffer. Instant gratification may displace concern for the next generation. People with short time horizons do not worry much about preparing children for the future. The broader lesson is that it is dangerous to draw sweeping conclusions on the basis of only one dimension of human behavior. It is just as misleading to predict human behavior solely on the basis of the instinct of parenthood as it is to predict human behavior solely on the basis of self-interest.

The instinct of workmanship is closely related to our parental bent and it also works for the common good. The instinct of workmanship can be defined as "a taste for effective work, and a distaste for futile effort" [Veblen, 1899, 15]. People have an instinctive affinity for efficiency and a dislike of waste; that affinity has helped the species to survive. There is an intrinsic joy associated with doing something useful. As most people know, not all work is painful. Most farmers get satisfaction from growing crops. Automobile mechanics feel a little pride when they make a repair. Professors are inwardly pleased when they deliver a good lecture. "Do-it yourself" projects are popular in part because people enjoy building and creating. That is not to say that work is always fun. It certainly is not. But we feel an intrinsic need to do something useful. As much as we like to "goof-off," most of us feel at least a little guilty about wasting time. We dislike pointless bureaucratic paper-pushing because it doesn't seem to accomplish anything useful; it is a waste of human effort.

The instinct of workmanship can be thought of as "the means by which the ends of parental bent are realized" [Diggins, 1977, 124]. In other words, the instinct of workmanship complements our parental bent because it supports the goal of producing things needed to care for the young. Veblen saw the two instincts as so closely related that it is "a matter of extreme difficulty to draw a line between them" [1914, 25]. But the instinct of workmanship also comes into play in the pursuit of the goals dictated by our other instincts. In fact, the instinct of workmanship "may in some sense be said to be auxiliary to all the rest" [Ibid. 31]. We get satisfaction from doing something constructive. Our other instincts provide the objectives that define what constructive means.

The third of the group-regarding instincts is what Veblen calls "idle curiosity." Idle curiosity is the idea that people "want to know things, when graver interests do not engross their attention" [Ibid. 85]. People are instinctively curious about their world. The idea that people are innately curious did not originate with Veblen, and is in fact very old. Aristotle, for example, begins his Metaphysics with the sentence, "All men by nature desire to know" [1984, 1552]. To be human is to wonder, to want know. We are a curious species.

The immediate reason we want to know is simple curiosity, with no utilitarian motive. As economic historian Joel Mokyr notes, "useful knowledge, more often than not, emerges before people know what it will be used for" [2002, 294]. The inventor of the laser, for example, was teased by his colleagues that his invention had no use, and was "a solution looking for a problem" [The Economist, 2005a, 25]. It now has an astonishingly large number of applications ranging from weapons to medical devices. Veblen points out that idle curiosity is often viewed as "a genial infirmity of human nature" [1914, 85]. Some people seem to have more idle curiosity than others, and those with a lot of it are often considered dreamers or even a little unbalanced [Ibid. 87]. Investigating something for no particular reason may seem like wasted energy, but the cumulative effect of many people "just wanting to know" is profound. Mokyr writes that "a lot results from curiosity, an essential human trait without which no historical theory of useful knowledge makes sense" [2002, 16]. Over the long term it is one of the most important forces in civilization. The simple curiosity of the species led to what Veblen called "the most substantial achievement of the race" [Ibid. 87], namely the systematic advancement of knowledge. In other words, idle curiosity is the root source of science, and of technological change.

Like other instincts, the extent to which idle curiosity manifests depends on a variety of factors. For one thing, idle curiosity finds an outlet only if people can afford to be idle. Only after needs such as food, clothing, shelter and reproduction have been met can one afford to spend time on something that has no immediate reward. It follows that the instinct of idle curiosity will be exercised more in economies with larger economic surpluses.

Idle curiosity and the instinct of workmanship, taken together, lead to improvements in technology. Idle curiosity leads to a better understanding of how the world works. The instinct of workmanship exploits the new knowledge to the extent that it leads to more efficient production methods. The better methods are also welcomed by our parental bent, as they make life easier for everyone. As we shall see, technological change is the primary catalyst for mutations in Veblen's evolutionary system. New technologies disturb the institutional structure, and can cause institutions to evolve.

In between the group-regarding and the purely self-regarding instincts is a gray area inhabited by the instinct of emulation. Veblen said that "the propensity for emulation - for invidious comparison - is of ancient growth and is a pervading trait of human nature" [1899, 109]. He goes so far as to say that, "with the exception of the instinct for self-preservation, the propensity for emulation is probably the strongest and most alert and persistent of the economic motives proper" [Ibid. 110]. People have a natural tendency to copy, to make comparisons and to rank the performances of others. Emulating others is how we learn. In choosing whom to emulate, we naturally decide that certain people are better at particular things than others.

We therefore come to rank people as better or worse, and we are aware that other people are ranking us. We become status-conscious creatures. We make "invidious comparisons," which means that we compare people and rank one person better than another. Invidious comparisons cause us to try to emulate those whom others praise, because we seek the status that comes from being ranked "better."

In many cases emulation is helpful to the group. For example, the instinct of workmanship causes people to appreciate hard work and efficiency. One can rank high in the esteem of the group if one can demonstrate a high degree of efficiency or craftsmanship. This may cause people to emulate the best workers and craftsmen so as to rank high in such invidious comparisons.

Emulation also played an important role in "what may well be the greatest shock to Western demographic history, namely the decline in infectious diseases in the industrialized West after 1870 or so." [Mokyr, 167]. Once scientists established the importance of cleanliness and soap, they had to convince the rest of the population. The first to be convinced were the high-status educated elite. Their high status made them objects of emulation, so the rest of the population was relatively quick to adopt the higher standards of hygiene. The result was better health for everyone.

But our propensity to emulate is not limited to socially beneficial behaviors. We are also capable of emulating self-regarding behaviors that do not advance the interests of the group, or that actually harm it. For example, many people throughout the world emulate gangsters. In the United States, the gangster subculture is the subject of popular music and movies. Suicide bombers emulate other suicide bombers. Emulation also plays a major role in consumption decisions, many of which are for the purpose of gaining or maintaining status. Fashions, for example, represent an endless quest to emulate the fashion leaders, who change fashions regularly. People do so because being "in fashion" affects one's social rank. But the quest absorbs resources that might be more useful to the group if devoted to other things.

The most obvious of the self-regarding instincts is self-preservation. It is a deep-seated instinct, common to all animals. It is likely that it is the most powerful of all instincts, but as countless acts of heroism large and small throughout history have demonstrated, it does not always override our parental bent. We have a strong desire to preserve our own lives, but not always at any cost.

Our proclivity for self-aggrandizement adds fuel to our tendency to make invidious comparisons, as we want to rank high in our social group. From an evolutionary standpoint, one might say that we want to be the leader of the pack, as that may aid our survival. In some situations self-aggrandizement may make us work harder to demonstrate our prowess. But it can take less helpful forms, as we may even do harm to others in order to improve our own standing. For example, self-aggrandizement can overwhelm parental instincts and can lead to the oppression of the young by the old. As Veblen wrote,

> The tutelage of the elders takes something of an authoritative tone and blends self-aggrandizement with their quasi-parental solicitude, giving an institutional outcome which makes the young generation subservient to the elders, ostensibly for the mutual and collective good of both parties to the relation; if predatory or warlike exploit in any degree becomes

habitual to the community the sentiment of self-aggrandizement gets the upper hand, and subservience
to the able-bodied elders becomes the dominant note
in this relation of tutelage, and their parental interest in the welfare of the incoming generation in a
corresponding degree goes into abeyance under the
pressure of the appropriate sentiments of pugnacity
and self-seeking, giving rise to a coercive regime of
a more or less ruthless character [1914, 45].

The subservience of the young to the old is common to many cultures, and would no doubt occur because of our parental bent alone.
After all, older people have more knowledge and wisdom than the
young. But when it is blended with self-aggrandizement, paternal-
ism can become an excuse for self-interested dominance. One need
only to look at the repressive dictatorships around the world to find
examples where self-aggrandizement is disguised as parental solici-
tude for the welfare of the masses.

Another of the self-regarding traits is our predatory instinct. The
predatory instinct is tied closely to our desire to rank high compared
to others. There is something in human nature that is gratified when
we can dominate other people. It is akin to the thrill of the hunt,
although in this case it is other people who are "hunted." We want
to demonstrate our superiority over others to "prove" our higher
status. Predatory actions may also allow us to get "something for
nothing."

The predatory instinct is exhibited in a variety of ways. In some
cultures, warfare is the most admired way of exercising predatory
drives. A victorious warrior demonstrates superior predatory prowess, and often brings home trophies as proof of his exploits. Tro-

phies may take the form of objects, which can range from useful goods to ceremonial paraphernalia. Trophies may also take the form of captives who are enslaved and forced to do the bidding of the warrior. As will be discussed in more detail in a later chapter, the use of low-status slaves to do useful labor is the beginning of a general association of productive work with "drudgery." The desire to rank high socially may therefore lead some to suppress their instinct of workmanship.

Another approach to predation is illustrated by what Veblen calls "the priestly class." Priests have high status by virtue of their close connection to the divinity. In addition, priests can claim that offerings are required to placate the divinity. Goods and status are extracted from others by the threat of divine retribution.

In a commercial culture such as ours, business and law take the place of warfare and religion as outlets for predatory tendencies. Consider the actions of a business that has a monopoly. In order to maximize profit, the monopolist will restrict output and raise price. Smaller output and higher price run contrary to the general interest of the public at large. But the monopolist does not mind exploiting its advantage at the expense of others.

The legal profession is frequently in the news for its predatory behavior. Popular jokes equate lawyers with sharks. Veblen wrote that "the lawyer is exclusively occupied with the details of predatory fraud, either in achieving or checkmating chicane" [1899, 231]. Lawyers use the power of their minds rather than the power of their arms, but their behavior is similar to that of warriors in that they seek to impose their will on others for their own benefit. The predatory instinct is still a part of human nature.

It is worth emphasizing that the instincts interact with each other. For example, the creation of a better weapon may involve the instincts of workmanship and idle curiosity, but the object of the improvement might be predatory. On the other hand, the desire for a better weapon could also arise from the instinct of parenthood, as the weapon may help protect the group. The point is that human drives are interrelated and easily blend into each other. No one instinct is always dominant; human nature is complex.

CHAPTER 2

INSTITUTIONS

It is almost a cliché, but people really are creatures of habit. As a result, humans have developed habitual ways to pursue the goals provided by their instincts. Individuals develop personal habits. Groups develop social conventions, which are no more than group habits. Over time, these habitual ways become deeply ingrained. They acquire a life of their own in the sense that they become the standard by which correct behavior and thinking are judged. Some are formalized as laws or rules. Others remain informal but retain a powerful hold over people as customs, traditions and reflexive habits of thought. All these habits, taken together, comprise a complex institutional structure. The institutions are interrelated and layered. They cover the entire range of human thought and activity. As Veblen put it, "institutions are habitual methods of carrying on the life process of the community" [1899, 193]. Almost everything we think and do is governed by habit.

It is almost impossible to overstate the importance of habit in Veblen's vision. Habitual behavior is pervasive, and governs how

we think and act. Habits have such control over us that we are often not even aware of them. Much of what we do that is "common
sense" is in fact done out of habit. It is worth quoting Veblen at
length on this point:

> The apparatus of ways and means available for the
> pursuit of whatever may be worth seeking is, sub-
> stantially all, a matter of tradition out of the past, a
> legacy of habits of thought accumulated through the
> experience of past generations. So that the manner,
> and in a great degree the measure, in which the in-
> stinctive ends of life are worked out under any given
> cultural situation is somewhat closely conditioned
> by these elements of habit ... . Under the discipline
> of habituation this logic and apparatus of ways and
> means falls into conventional lines, acquires the con-
> sistency of custom and prescription, and so takes on
> an institutional character and force. The accustomed
> ways of doing and thinking not only become an ha-
> bitual matter of course, easy and obvious, but they
> come likewise to be sanctioned by social convention,
> and so become right and proper and give rise to prin-
> ciples of conduct. By use and wont they are incorpo-
> rated into the scheme of common sense [1914, 6-7].

Most habits of thought and behavior are inherited from the past
as traditions. We acquire them as we grow up and are taught how
to behave and how to think. We become "socialized" by learning
what our family, community and nation consider to be right and
wrong. As children we are taught religion, views on politics, how to
dress, what to eat, how to behave in public, the proper roles of men
and women in society, views on race, the proper upkeep of a yard,

and a host of other things great and small. The views we are taught become our view of what is true, right and even natural.

We may acquire different views later in life, but habits of thought, whenever acquired, are difficult to change. The primary reason for the durability of habits of thought is that individuals generally do not acquire them as the result of any reasoning process. They are not the result of any rational calculation. Rather, all "right thinking" people are led to understand that the views held by our family and community are true and right. Most people in the U.S. would never even think about eating a dog because we reflexively "know" that it is wrong and inhumane. Yet in other parts of the world, eating a dog is acceptable. Most people in the U.S. do not think twice about eating a cow or a pig, but in some parts of the world that would be an abomination.

The pressure to conform to society's norms is enormous. Violations of formal institutions such as laws and rules carry formal sanctions such as fines, prison and job loss. Violations of informal institutions such as dressing strangely or eating the wrong food can result in social isolation or worse. Social sanctions force most people to conform. As Veblen put it, "only individuals with an aberrant temperament can in the long run retain their self-esteem in the face of the disesteem of their fellows" [1899, 30]. Consequently, institutions are inherently conservative. Few people want to risk the penalties associated with acting contrary to what everyone else "knows" to be proper. We don't dare walk outside naked, even on a hot summer day, because the neighbors will think we are crazy, and we might get arrested. In fact, our habits of thought are so deeply ingrained that most people cannot even conceive of acting contrary to established conventions. When was the last time you thought about cooking up some insects for dinner, even though many of them have high nutritional value?

Informal habits of thought are often more powerful than formal laws. Consider, for example, two common traffic laws. One law requires all motorists to stop at red lights while another requires motorists to obey the speed limit. The first law is almost universally obeyed, and people will wait patiently for the light to change even when there are no other cars in sight. The second law is frequently violated, and most people don't feel the least bit guilty about doing so. The difference lies in motorists' habits of thought. Speed limits are commonly viewed as too restrictive and so are often ignored.

Habitual behavior no doubt evolved because it is a way for us to deal with complexity. Every day we face a myriad of decisions including what to eat, what to wear, how fast to drive, how to communicate and what to think about world events. Habit and convention simplify our lives by giving us reflexive, automatic answers to most of these questions. If we had to reflect on each and every decision we would be paralyzed or insane in short order. We typically stop to reflect only when confronted with something unfamiliar for which there is no habitual or conventional response.

Habitual behavior embodied in institutions serves the important function of organizing society. Consider what would happen if every individual had a different view of the "right" way to do things. Chaos and conflict would result. Social order requires some degree of consensus. Institutions allow us to agree on how we should organize activities at all levels, from the family to the nation (or even the world). What would happen if there were no conventions regarding language? How would we communicate? Making everyone drive on the same side of the road makes traffic flow smoother and reduces accidents. The habit of brushing one's teeth every day reduces the problem of tooth decay. Setting standards as to how electricity should be delivered allows us to mass-produce electric appliances. The universal acceptance of intrinsically worthless pieces of paper in payment for goods and services facilitates trade. All of these institutions help individuals and society solve real problems. Without institutions, civilization could not exist.

But to say that institutions organize society does not imply that society is organized in the "best" possible way or that all institutions serve a useful purpose.[4] Some institutions have no real purpose, and are more or less innocuous. A number of superstitions fall into this category, such as the habit of avoiding black cats. Or consider the practice of throwing rice at a wedding. The rice symbolizes fertility, but most everyone knows that throwing rice has no effect whatsoever on the couple's fertility. Another example is the expectation that men in the United States must wear ties to any "formal" occasion. The tie serves no purpose other than to meet a traditional requirement. In fact, wearing a tie may even be harmful, as there is some evidence that ties can restrict the flow of blood to the head. But even though an institution such as wearing a tie does not solve any real problem, people take it very seriously. If a man shows up at a formal event in the "wrong" clothes, he will be criticized for not having the proper respect for the event, and then ostracized or told to leave.

Other institutions are more sinister in that they act to preserve social hierarchies, encourage invidious behavior, or are harmful in other ways. The severe restrictions placed on women until recently in the West and in some other cultures today are examples of how institutions can establish and preserve social hierarchies. Keeping women illiterate, for example, makes them easier to control. Habits of thought regarding race, nationality and religion rank people from "better" to "worse." In medieval Europe it was believed that one's social status was divinely ordained, and that the king ruled by divine right. A modern example of an institution that harms everyone is the belief that that the polio vaccine is a Western device to make Africans sterile. That belief is the primary reason why polio has not been eradicated, and causes many people to suffer unnecessarily [Economist, 2004a].

In Veblen's mind, one of the most harmful habits of thought is nationalism. Nationalism stems from the deeply held belief that artificial political boundaries divide Us from Them. Nationalism necessarily carries with it an invidious ranking of people, with those of other nationalities considered less worthy or less human. Politicians and others exploit nationalism for their own advantage. One result is war. As will be discussed later, businessmen take advantage of nationalism to further their interests at the expense of the community's. Veblen expressed his deep distaste for nationalism as follows:

> Born in iniquity and conceived in sin, the spirit of nationalism has never ceased to bend human institutions to the service of dissension and distress. In its material effects it is altogether the most sinister as well as the most imbecile of all those institutional incumbrances that have come down out of the old order. The national mob-mind of vanity, fear, hate, contempt, and servility still continues to make loyal citizens a con-

> venient tool in the hands of the Adversary, whether
> these sentiments cluster about the anointed person of
> a sovereign or about the magic name of the Republic.
> Within a fraction of one per cent., the divine right
> of the Nation has the same size, shape, color, and
> density as the divine right the Stuart kings once had,
> or as the divine right of Bourbons, Hapsburgers and
> Hohenzollern have continued to have at a later date;
> and it has also the same significance for "life, liberty
> and the pursuit of happiness" [1923, 38-9].

Unfortunately, the scourge of nationalism is still with us.

Many, if not most, institutions actually combine useful and not so useful functions. For example, people wear clothes in order to protect themselves from the elements. That function could be accomplished with very simple and inexpensive garments. But people often choose to wear expensive clothes that are "in fashion," and are willing to buy new clothes every time fashions change. People do so because they feel that they must in order to maintain their social status. Or consider the previously mentioned habit of brushing one's teeth regularly. The habit has the useful function of reducing tooth decay, but people also do it to meet the social custom that requires white teeth and "fresh" breath.

Habits may begin as ways to solve problems, but as they solidify into institutions, they take on a life of their own. People are expected to observe the institution not for its usefulness, but because "right-thinking" individuals "know" that it is the right thing to do. If you ask most people why they mow the grass in their yards, they will tell you that one is just supposed to. If pressed, they may say that the grass looks nicer mown, or that they have to mow it in order to keep up appearances and property values. Mowing the grass has become almost purely ceremonial. People do it because they are expected to. Yet the habit has practical roots. Tall grass is a favored habitat of vermin such as ticks. Keeping the grass short reduces the chances of getting tick-borne diseases. But this practical purpose has been lost in the status-seeking competition to have the greenest, most weed-free, best-trimmed lawn on the block. Actions first taken to protect health have turned into the Cult of the Lawn.

Institutions persist because of the power of habit and tradition. We accept them because they seem "normal" or even "good" to us. They are inherited from the past and are internalized as right and true. And the older the tradition, the more normal it seems. It is easy to look at new ideas or at alien cultures and see their flaws, but it is difficult to do so with "time-honored" traditions in our own culture. We are taught from infancy to view our traditions as normal and natural, so we rarely, if ever, subject them to rational thought. If we do think about them and decide that they are wrong, it is still very hard to change them because of the penalties associated with violating accepted laws, rules or customs. Working against accepted conventions often requires an extraordinary amount of courage, and success is rare.

It is important to emphasize the tenacity of institutions. Consider the following story about a habit that persisted long after it no longer served any useful purpose:

> At the outset of World War II, Britain was still scrounging for any weapons it could get its hands on, and so de-mothballed a piece of light field artillery from the Boer War. The five-man crew it rounded up

had a curious system for firing the armament: Precisely three seconds prior to discharging the gun, two of the men would snap to attention until all was silent again. None of the experts or young officers consulted could deduce the point of the exercise. Finally, they brought in a wizened retired artillery colonel. He watched the exercise for a moment, then, jarred by an old memory, recognition flickered in his eyes: "I have it. They are holding the horses." You see, in the past those two men would have physically held the horses to prevent them from running off with the sound of the cannon [Goldberg, 2005, 6].

The "right" way to fire the gun persisted long after the horses were no longer used.

If habits of thought with no purpose can persist for so long, imagine the resistance to change of an institution that benefits one group at the expense of another. "Vested interests" do not easily give away their advantages. To take just one example, men benefited from the subjugation of women, so they had no incentive to change. Women were rarely in a position to insist on change, even if they thought about it. After all, they were raised to view their role in society as perfectly normal. Women in the United States were not given the right to vote until 1920. Even today, habits of thought about the "proper" role of women in society are not uniformly "modern."

In Veblen's evolutionary scheme, institutions are the equivalent of genetic material. They are the means by which a society replicates itself from generation to generation. If genes were radically different from one generation to the next, it is likely that the species would not be able to survive. Stable genes make for a stable species. Likewise, the stability of institutions means that societies are stable from generation to generation. In a general sense, it is good that institutions resist change. If they were completely flexible, society would descend into chaos and might not survive. But like genes, institutions are subject to mutation. They can change. The changes are typically small, but the effect of many small changes over time can be quite large.

Even in "revolutions," most institutions stay the same. Habits of thought do not change overnight just because there is a new type of government. When revolutionary governments try to change too much too fast, most people resist. If the new rulers insist on change, it can only be accomplished by force. Tens of millions died when Soviet and Chinese Communist zealots insisted on dramatic, rapid, revolutionary change.

Veblen's primary objective was to explain how and why institutions evolve. In contrast to the neoclassical obsession with static equilibria, Veblen wanted to explain the process of change. His goal was to create a theory of evolutionary economics along Darwinian lines. The most obvious feature of a modern economy is the fact that it is never in equilibrium and is constantly changing. Moreover, the rate of change seems to be accelerating. Veblen wanted to know why.

PART II
TECHNOLOGY AND SOCIAL EVOLUTION

So what causes institutions to change, and why has the pace of change increased in the past few centuries? The short answer is that technological change is the primary cause of institutional change, and the faster the rate of technological change, the faster the pace of institutional change. Technological change can create new possibilities and new problems that put pressure on institutions to change. At a more fundamental level, the process of technological change can affect how we think. That, in turn, can affect how we view our institutions. But before looking at these ideas in more detail, it is worthwhile to consider the nature of technology.

CHAPTER 3

TECHNOLOGY

Contrary to neoclassical parables about Robinson Crusoe-economies, humans live in groups. Veblen wrote that "in the economic respect man has never lived an isolated, self-sufficient life as an individual, either actually or potentially. Humanly speaking, such a thing is impossible" [1919, 324]. Even the famously independent "mountain men" of early American history would rendezvous once a year to barter for goods they needed but could not make themselves. The amount of knowledge needed to provide even a "primitive" standard of living is too extensive for a single individual to possess. Technology, even in primitive groups, is possessed and transmitted by the group as a whole. As Veblen put it,

> Information and proficiency in the ways and means of life vests in the group at large; and apart from accretions borrowed from other groups, it is the product of the given group, though not produced by any single generation ... and it can also be maintained and retained only by the community at large. Whatever may be true for the unsearchable prehistoric phases of the

life-history of the race, it appears to be true for the most primitive human groups that the mass of techno-logical knowledge possessed by any community, and necessary for its maintenance and to the maintenance of each of its members or subgroups, is too large a burden for any one individual or any single line of descent to carry. This holds true, all the more rigor-ously and consistently, the more advanced the "state of the industrial arts" may be [1919, 325-6].

Veblen read extensively in the area of anthropology and knew that the amount of knowledge possessed by "primitive" communi-ties was far greater than what most "modern" people suspect. But even if that weren't true, nobody can dispute the fact that the amount of knowledge possessed by modern societies far exceeds the capac-ity of any individual or family.

To illustrate how even a "simple" bit of modern technology requires far more knowledge than any one person has, consider an ordinary number two pencil.[5] To make a pencil one must have knowledge of how to find and transport the necessary materials: graphite and clay to make the "lead," metal ores to make the eraser holder, rubber for the eraser, pigments and chemicals for the paint and wood for the body of the pencil. Then one must know how to properly use the materials to produce the desired results. Of course, one would also have to know how to make the tools needed to do all of these things, and how to make the tools needed to make the tools. No one individual or family knows how to do all of these things. And a pencil is considered "low-tech."

The point is that individuals know only a tiny fraction of all that a society knows. The more sophisticated the technology, the smaller the fraction any one individual can know. In addition, an individual's knowledge is generally of value only in the context of society. Our individual specialized bits of knowledge are valuable only because others know things that complement what we know. Take a few of the most advanced scientists and engineers on the planet and put them in the midst of a stone-age tribe. Without an army of modern workers and technicians to help them, their advanced knowledge would be largely useless. In fact, unless they were given appropriate training, the scientists and engineers would probably be a liability to the tribe.

The fact that modern legal institutions allow individuals to patent pieces of knowledge does not change the communal nature of technology. A particular pharmaceutical company, for example, may be the only one that knows how to make a particular drug. But without the knowledge possessed by the people who make and transport the requisite ingredients and equipment, and without the knowledge of the people who make the tools needed to make the ingredients, equipment, and transportation, the patent would be useless.

A corollary to the idea that technology is a group possession is the fact that breaking up the group can diminish or destroy its technology [Veblen, 1914, 110]. As already mentioned, knowledge held by isolated individuals is of little value. It follows that a loss of group cohesion can be detrimental to its technology. The Aztec calendar was astonishingly accurate, but the technology needed to produce it disappeared soon after the Spanish conquest. The social fragmentation that accompanied the disintegration of the Roman Empire insured that much useful knowledge would be lost, and it took a long time for Europe to recover. Any major social dislocation will have a similar effect.

A society's technology is, from an economic standpoint, its most valuable possession. Technology, or what Veblen called a society's "immaterial equipment," [1915, 272] is far more valuable than material equipment. In a passage about the California Indians, Veblen wrote that

> the loss of the basket, digging stick, and mortar, simply as physical objects, would have signified little, but the conceivable loss of the squaw's knowledge of the soil and the seasons, of food and fiber plants, and of mechanical expedients would have meant the present dispersal and starvation of the community [Ibid. 185].

With the right knowledge, lost material equipment can be replaced. Without knowledge, we are incapable of producing anything. Moreover, without the knowledge of how to use them, the most advanced machines and equipment are useless.

It follows that if a society can maintain its cohesion and therefore retain its technology, it can withstand much devastation. A war might destroy a nation's factories and infrastructure, but as long as the society is intact, it can recover. Its technology will allow it to replace the lost material equipment. Knowledge is far more important than material possessions.

Many have commented on the ability of countries to recover from very destructive wars or from natural disasters. The rapid recoveries of Japan and German from the utter devastation of World War II have been described as miraculous. Japan's per capita GDP, for example, was less than 20 percent of U.S. per capita GDP in 1950, but was over 80 percent of U.S. per capita GDP by 1991 [Cox and Koo, 2006, 1]. Germany's speedy recovery spawned the term Wirtschaftswunder [Economist, 2006, 3]. But the recoveries only appeared miraculous because of an inability to see that knowledge of the industrial arts matters far more than material equipment. There is a bias in the way economists and others see the world. Material equipment is tangible and can be valued. People can see the effect of a war or an earthquake on factories and houses, and a dollar estimate of the destruction can be made. On the other hand, technology, the "immaterial equipment," cannot be seen and cannot be measured. If a war destroys every physical structure, the nation will appear to have lost everything. But unless the human casualties are extraordinarily high, it will retain its most valuable possession, its knowledge.

> Immaterial equipment is, far and away, the more important productive agency in the case; although, it is true, economists have not been in the habit of making much of it, since it is in the main not capable of being stated in terms of price, and so does not appear in the statistical schedules of accumulated wealth [Veblen, 1915, 272].

If something cannot be measured in dollars, it tends to be ignored by economists and accountants. But it is a mistake to conclude that it isn't valuable. As the old saying puts it, "not everything that counts can be counted."

It is fashionable to describe the modern economy as the "knowledge economy." The truth is that all economies are knowledge economies. Knowledge is at the core of everything we have and do. We may measure the wealth of nations by the dollar volume of goods and services produced, or by stocks of tangible assets, but their real wealth is their technology. The point is often overlooked in part because technology cannot be conveniently measured.

The critical importance of technology means that it is worthwhile to examine the process of technological change. As previously mentioned, the instinct of idle curiosity is responsible for the discovery of much new knowledge. The fact that some individuals tend to have an unusually large amount of idle curiosity (and idle time) may seem to imply that technological change is an individual phenomenon. But that is an illusion. Individuals live in groups, and draw their existing knowledge from the group's pool of knowledge. In addition, the individual's habits of thought are conditioned by group life. As Veblen wrote,

> Each successive advance, every new wrinkle of novelty, improvement, invention, adaptation, every further detail of workmanlike innovation, is of course made by individuals and comes out of individual experience and initiative, since the generations of mankind live only in individuals. But each move so made is necessarily made by individuals immersed in the community and exposed to the discipline of group life as it runs in the community, since all life is necessarily group life [1914, 103-4].

Robinson Crusoe could not have invented the microchip.

An individual can know only a tiny fraction of the total stock of knowledge. That means that knowledge is specialized. One person may know things that another person doesn't, and vice versa. As knowledge becomes more specialized, each of us becomes more dependent on the group. But we also have the opportunity to delve deeper into our narrow area of expertise. As the old joke has it, we know more and more about less and less. The increased specialization is conducive to expanding our understanding of the topic at hand. We can focus our attention and so gain a greater understanding of our specialized area.

In book one, chapter three of *The Wealth of Nations*, Adam Smith [1776] explained that the degree of specialization in production is limited by the extent of the market. Specialization increases worker productivity, but if the increased output cannot be sold, there is no point in specializing. Only a large market will allow for extensive specialization. Veblen made an analogous argument with respect to the specialization of knowledge. One cannot become a narrow specialist in a small community. If you are the only doctor, you cannot specialize in heart disease; you have to treat everything. Specialization becomes possible only when the community is large enough to support many doctors. As a result, it is unlikely that a doctor in a small community can make a deep study of heart disease and make advances in how to treat it.

The point is that the size of the technological community has a profound impact on the rate of technological change. A small, isolated community is not likely to advance very quickly. It is worth quoting Veblen at length on this point:

> This necessary specialisation and detail training has large consequences for the growth of technology as well as for its custody and transmission. It follows that a large and widely diversified industrial scheme is impossible except in a community of some size - large enough to support a number and variety of special occupations. In effect, substantial gains in

> industrial insight and proficiency can apparently be worked out only through such close and sustained attention to a given line of work as can be given only within the lines of a specialised occupation. At the same time the industrial community must comprise a full complement of such specialised occupations, and must also be bound together in a system of communication sufficiently close and facile to allow the technological contents of all these occupations to be readily assimilated into a systematic whole ... . If the degree of isolation is pronounced, so that traffic and communication do not run freely between groups, the size of the local group will limit the state of the industrial arts somewhat rigidly [1914, 107-8].

Veblen emphasized that "community" in this case refers to a technological community, not to a political community. He noted that a small country with a small population can be part of a large technological community if it engages in open and free communication with other countries [Ibid. 109n]. To the extent that a country is isolated, it will experience a decline in its rate of technological change. Writing just prior to the outbreak of World War I, Veblen predicted that technological advancement would be retarded by "the efforts of those patriotic and dynastic statesmen who are endeavouring to set these people asunder in an armed estrangement" [Ibid. 109n]. Even in times of peace, political boundaries tend to impede the flow of communication and thereby slow the rate of technological change. Nationalism impedes the economic development of humanity.

Instincts also shape technological change. Idle curiosity may generate new ideas, but how those ideas are used depends on the goals established by the other instincts. Where warlike predatory tendencies dominate, new ideas are likely to be considered in light of their ability to help build new weapons. Where parental instincts dominate, more nurturing applications will be sought. Atomic theory gave us both nuclear weapons and medical treatments.

Instincts will guide technological change to the extent that "the growth of institutions has not seriously diverted the genius of the race from its natural bent" [Veblen, Ibid. 110]. Institutions shape both how new ideas are used and the direction of technological change. Existing habits of thought use new technology to support existing institutions. It is no coincidence that the first book Johann Gutenberg published with his moveable type was a Bible. The most powerful formal institution in the West at that time was the Christian religion, and the new technology was put to work in its service. Other uses of the printing press were restricted, especially those that might challenge religious or political authority. Even today, the freedom to use printing technology is severely curtailed in many parts of the world because it is a threat to established habits of thought and institutions. The power of what Veblen called "vested interests" to limit or control new technology is enormous.

Institutions sometimes cause people to make use of new technology in surprising and disturbing ways. Modern technology allows one to determine the sex of an unborn child. In China, that ability, coupled with laws prohibiting couples from having more than one child, has led to many selective abortions of female fetuses. That is because traditionally, males are preferred to females. The result is a growing imbalance between the number of males and females in the country. China's 2000 census reported 118 boys born for every 100 girls, compared to a normal ratio of 105 to 100 [Economist, 2004b].

The long run demographic effects could be profound.

Habits of thought shape the use of technology by defining which technologies are "good" and which are "bad". In the institution known as business, good and bad are defined as profit and loss. New technologies that increase profits are welcomed while those that do not are shunned. Religion also helps define "good" and "bad" technology. Amish people do not use electricity. Islamic terrorists decry Western decadence but use modern communication technology to transmit videos of them beheading people in the name of their predatory feudal cause. The same people prohibit women from driving. The use of technology is often allowed only when it furthers the objectives of institutions.

Institutions also affect which technologies will be pursued. Modern lines of inquiry into such things as genetic engineering, cloning and stem cell research have been curtailed by ethical and religious habits of thought. Business habits of thought control the modern economy and so have a large role in shaping technological development. Technologies that promise to increase profits are sought; those that are unprofitable but might be "good" according to non-business institutions are not pursued. We encourage things we consider "good" and discourage things we consider "bad," but good and bad are defined by the institutional structure.

At an even more basic level, institutions affect technological change because systems of knowledge are themselves habits of thought. Veblen described the "state of the industrial arts" as "a system of habits of thought" [Veblen, 1915, 272]. What we "know" to be true about the world is conditioned by habitual thinking. We examine new ideas and observations in the context of our habitual method of thinking. Ptolemy's theory that the earth was the center of the universe survived for 1400 years. New discoveries about the movement of the stars and planets were made to fit into Ptolemy's system because people habitually looked at the universe from a geocentric point of view. The force of habit was so great that it was almost impossible to think in any other terms.

Every modern field of inquiry has an habitual way of looking at the world. Every "school of thought" is just a set of conventions through which new ideas are filtered. Specialists in every field are taught a particular approach, and most are incapable of thinking about the world in any other way. The few that can rise above the conventional wisdom are inhibited by the penalties that face anyone who violates an institution. "Heretics" are rarely burned at the stake anymore in the West, but one's employment and reputation are put at risk by unorthodox views. In contrast, there are rewards for not rocking the boat. As Veblen accurately observed, "the well-worn paths are easy to follow and lead into good company" [1919, 79].

Even if there were no penalties for holding unorthodox views, such views are themselves just another set of conventions. Those who manage to escape the orthodoxy soon develop their own habitual ways of looking at the world. The only difference between an orthodox and an unorthodox approach to a field of inquiry is a disagreement about which habitual mode of thinking is correct. In both cases the inquiry is constrained by an habitual world-view. There is no escaping the fact that people are creatures of habit.

Institutions affect the speed and direction of technological change. But technological change, in turn, affects the speed and direction of institutional change. In fact, technological change is the primary catalyst for institutional change. It is the source of mutations in the genetic material that makes up a society. As Veblen wrote,

> There are two lines of agency visibly at work shaping the habits of thought of the people ... . These are the received scheme of use and wont, and the new state of the industrial arts; and it is not difficult to see that it is the latter that makes for readjustment; nor should it be any more difficult to see that the readjustment is necessarily made under the surveillance of the received scheme of use and wont [1915, 72].

The "new state of the industrial arts" (new technology) can disturb "the received scheme of use and wont" (the institutional structure). The changes initiated by new technology are, however, guided by the existing institutions.

CHAPTER 4

TECHNOLOGICAL CHANGE AND INSTITUTIONAL CHANGE

When a new technology emerges, existing institutions do not prescribe how individuals or the society should employ it. Because it is new, there are no habits or conventions governing its use. It is only after the fact that institutions arise to govern the use of the new technology. For example, the automobile existed before there were any laws or conventions governing how it would be used. But as automobiles became popular, it became obvious that predictable patterns of use were needed to avoid accidents and to improve traffic flow. Traffic laws were created. Now, one can legally drive only after reaching a certain age and demonstrating knowledge of the laws. In other words, automobile technology generated new institutions, and as a result, use of the technology came to be governed by the new institutions.

New technologies often do more than just generate new institutions; they also alter or destroy old institutions. Technological change brings with it social change. For example, the technologies that led to the factory system altered how and where we worked. As Mokyr wrote,

> Much of the history of technological revolutions in the past two centuries is written as if the only things that technology affected were output, productivity, and economic welfare as approximated by income. ... Yet technological progress also affected other aspects of the economy that may be significant. Among those is the optimal scale of the basic economic production unit and the location where production takes place. These in turn determine whether "work" will be carried out in a specialized location and thus whether households and firms will be separate entities [2002, 119-20].

As production technology advanced, the amount of knowledge one needed to use it came to exceed what a single person or family could grasp, even in a specialized line of work. There was "information overload" [Mokyr, 2202, 139]. As Veblen wrote, "machine industry calls for a large-scale organisation" [1914, 351]. The independent producer could not compete with production organized in a factory. The shift to factory production demolished ancient habits. For one thing, most people no longer worked at home. Family life changed dramatically as one or more adults spent most of the day away from home. Time and energy were spent travelling to and from work. Workers were no longer their own bosses, and so could not choose how many hours to work each day. And workers who had always worked in their own homes and at their own pace "had to be taught to follow orders, to respect the space and property rights of others, and to be punctual, docile, and sober" [Mokyr, 2002, 129].

Teaching workers to be "punctual" presupposes the existence of an accurate clock. The clock has regimented human life to an extent that was impossible before the technology that made clocks possible. Veblen said that "the discipline of the timepiece" is "a fact of the first importance" [1914, 312]. Habitual behavior based on " 'apparent' solar time" [Ibid.] gave way to behavior based on time as defined by a clock. We go to work at the same time on both the winter and the summer solstice, even when our bodies object.

Automobile technology also had a dramatic impact on how we live. Among other things, it completely changed the traditional conception of a community. By increasing the ease and speed of travel, people were able to move from densely populated cities to less densely populated suburbs. In a densely populated neighborhood, one must regularly interact with many other people. In a low-density suburb, one is more isolated and ties to others in the neighborhood are weak. The automobile also changed our courtship rituals, how we shop, and where we go for recreation. Very few aspects of life were untouched by the automobile.

Such far-reaching changes do not happen overnight. The "rehabituation of the people and the gradual readjustment of legal and moral conceptions" [Veblen, 1915, 101] takes time. As mentioned earlier, institutions are inherently conservative. Habits of thought persist even when they are obviously out of date. Resistance to advancements in medicine after 1800 was fierce because so much of it ran counter to received medical wisdom and habitual practices [Mokyr, 2002, 266]. The tenacity of old ideas meant that many people died needlessly. One anecdote may serve to illustrate the point:

> When President Garfield was shot, sixteen years after the introduction of antisepsis, the numerous physicians who saw him did not think twice before poking his wound with their finger. The Surgeon General of the Navy introduced his finger to its full extent into the wound, as did Dr. J. J. Woodward and a Dr. Bliss, two physicians present. A homeopathic physician who rushed into the room added a deep finger-poke of his own. It is not surprising that Garfield died not of the shot itself but from infection and complications ten weeks after the incident [Mokyr, 2002, 226n].

Medical science by that time knew enough to take basic precautions against infection. Reputable physicians always attend the President of the United States. But reputation is often established by mastery of time-honored methods, not new-fangled ideas. The "best" physicians in the country resisted new medical knowledge and it killed a president.

The broader point is that because habits of thought and institutions are handed down from the past, they can never be in complete harmony with the present technology. As Veblen put it, "institutions are products of past process, are adapted to past circumstances, and are therefore never in full accord with the requirements of the present" [1899, 191]. Medical practices learned in the past reflect past methods, not present knowledge. It is a cliché that generals are always fighting the last war; their thinking has not adjusted to new military technology. The paperless world made possible by new information technology has not materialized in part because people are accustomed to reading words printed on paper, not computer screens. Technological change may eventually change habits of thought, but it is always with a lag.

At a more fundamental level, technological change alters how people think about the world in general. The process of creating or using a new technology involves matter-of-fact, cause-and-effect thinking. It leaves little room for superstition and traditional taboos. Learning how to use an MP3 player does not require one to defer to any ancient tradition; one simply wants to know the easiest and most efficient way to obtain the desired result. The MP3 player may even be used to listen to music that glorifies a major traditional institution such as a nation or a religion. Nevertheless, the process of learning how to use it gives a boost to cause-and-effect thinking, which is the opposite of traditional thinking. One does not ask if MP3 players are usable only by certain age groups, require a license, or need a special blessing from a religious authority. A new technology has no ceremonial baggage. Its most efficient use is all that matters.

The concern for efficiency embodied in cause-and-effect thinking may lead some to look at habitual ways of doing things and to ask if there might be a better way to do them. If one is exposed to new technology repeatedly, one might even develop the habit of thinking about the world in a cause-and-effect fashion. That makes it easier to question habitual ways of doing things and so makes institutions easier to change. The technological, workmanlike approach "becomes not only the instrument of inquiry in the sciences, but a major premise in all work of innovation and reconstruction of the scheme of institutions" [Veblen, 1914, 285-6]. Habituation to cause-and-effect thinking spills over into thinking about existing institutions, and leads some to ask if the current institutions are necessary or well-suited to dealing with current problems. In an industrial setting, engineers are primarily interested in solving problems as efficiently as possible. They may become annoyed when institutional arrangements make that difficult. Almost anyone who has ever worked for a large organization has chaffed at rules that make solving problems difficult. The natural response is to ask why institutions have to be the way they are, and to ask if they could be changed for the better.

The effect of technological change on how people think is not uniform across the population. For example, Veblen distinguishes between industrial employments (such as engineering and factory work) and pecuniary employments (such as business and law) [1904, 314]. Workers in industrial occupations routinely work with machines. There is no room for superstition; one must learn to think in a cause-and–effect manner. Workers in pecuniary occupations do not generally come in direct contact with the discipline of the machine, and hence are less affected by it. They are affected to some degree, as they may manage or direct industrial concerns. But they are primarily concerned about making money, not about industrial technology. A belief in "luck" may be part of pecuniary occupations, but there is very little room for luck in engineering. Engineers may therefore be more likely than lawyers to seek efficient institutions.

The very wealthy are sheltered altogether from the necessity of work, and so are not routinely exposed to new ideas and technologies or the habits of thought that go with them [Veblen, 1899, 193]. The fact that they do not have to work means that they can safely ignore new habits of thought. Unlike industrial workers, "they are not required under penalty of forfeiture to change their habits of life and their theoretical views of the external world to suit the demands of an altered industrial technique, since they are not in the full sense an organic part of the industrial community" [Ibid. 198]. The high status of the wealthy means that others will emulate their actions and attitudes. Their status "makes it incumbent on all reputable people to follow their lead" [Ibid. 200]. The wealthy can cling to old ideas and institutions without penalty, and others admire them for it. The result is that institutional change is slowed.

Professors are another group that generally faces little pressure to change their "theoretical views of the external world." If tenured professors are wrong about something, they can go on being wrong for as long as they like. They will not lose their jobs or take a cut in pay. Attachment to wrong or obsolete ideas is even encouraged if there are large numbers of like-minded people in the same discipline. Adam Smith observed that many universities "have chosen to remain, for a long time, the sanctuaries in which exploded systems and obsolete prejudices found shelter and protection, after they had been hunted out of every other corner of the world" [1776, 772]. Smith's observation is still too often true.

Despite the conservative habits of thought of the wealthy and of professors, technological change applies constant pressure to institutions. Even if we are not forced to confront new technology in our work, we are likely to do so as consumers. The cumulative effect is that technological change alters how we live and challenges how we see the world. Writing about the modern age, Veblen wrote that "the machine discipline acts to disintegrate the institutional heritage, of all degrees of antiquity and authenticity" [1904, 374].

It should be stressed that while Veblen saw technological change as the main cause of institutional change, he did not argue that it was the only cause, or that it determined what the new institutions would be like. He was not a technological determinist. As Brette [2003] observed, "institutional change appears, in Veblen's work, as the unpredictable outcome of dynamic interactions between technical, instinctive and institutional factors" [472].

Recall that technological change arises because of the instinct of idle curiosity and the instinct of workmanship. At the same time, the other instincts influence the direction of technological change. Moreover, whether group or self regarding instincts dominate depends to a large degree on the institutional structure. Warlike habits of thought direct technological change along predatory lines. Nurturing habits of thought allow the parental bent to guide technological development so as to benefit humanity as a whole. Thus, technological change is shaped by the institutional structure.

Institutions are interrelated. As Veblen put it, "culture...is a balanced system of habits, essentially habits of thought" [1915, 221]. If one institution changes, other institutions will be affected. In addition, the logic of the dominant institutions makes itself felt throughout the web of interrelated institutions. This logic, or "central conventions" [Rutherford, 1984, 335] puts pressure on other institutions to change so as to conform to the dominant habits of thought. For example, in the modern era, business is the dominant institution. Business thinking conditions us to value things according to their pecuniary (monetary) value. It is no surprise that Christmas has become increasingly commercialized. The tradition of gift giving is very old, but that does not explain why a spiritual holiday has turned into an orgy of materialism. Expressions of love, under pressure from commercial habits of thought, have been reduced to an exchange of expensive goods.

Veblen provided an extensive analysis of another example in his book The Higher Learning in America [1918]. The ostensible purpose of universities and colleges is to create and to transmit knowledge. But they are part of the broader culture, and are not immune to the logic of business. Veblen wrote that

> These pecuniary conditions that impose themselves on the processes of industry and on the conduct of life, together with the pecuniary accountancy that goes with them - the price system - have much to say in the guidance and limitations of workmanship. And when and in so far as the habituation so enforced in the traffic of workday life goes into effect as a scheme of logic governing the quest for knowledge, such principles as have by habit found acceptance as being conventionally salutary and conclusive in the pecuniary conduct of affairs will necessarily leave their mark on the ideals, aims, methods and standards of science and scholarship [1918, 6].

It should be no surprise that colleges now routinely evaluate the merits of programs of study in terms of revenue and cost.

The more general point is that institutional structures have their own internal logic which manifest as habits of thought. These deep-seated habits are used without reflection to evaluate all institutions. The process may sometimes be slow, but inexorably, institutions that do not conform to the central conventions will be altered. A technological change may directly create or affect a small number of institutions, but the changes will reverberate throughout the entire institutional scheme. A disturbance of the "balanced system of habits" can set in motion changes that cannot be predicted.

Veblen's objective was to construct a theory of the process of institutional change "stated in terms of the process itself" [1919, 77]. In other words, he wanted a theory of change that did not rely on exogenous forces. By emphasizing the dynamic interaction of instincts, institutions and technology, he sought to endogenize the process. But that does not mean that he ruled out the possibility that exogenous shocks could alter the institutional structure. Such shocks include actions taken by other societies, including war, as well as "environmental shifts" [Jennings and Waller, 1994, 1002]. A significant change in the environment can lead to substantial change in human societies. Recall that in a previous chapter it was noted that during the most recent ice age, there was a strong selection process that favored co-operative behavior over individualistic behavior. The climate change that is now under way may necessitate an even higher level of cooperation.

It is worth remembering that social evolution, no matter what the source, does not guarantee "progress." How cultures change is unpredictable; change can be for the better and for the worse. Moreover, institutions are remarkably resilient. As Veblen put it, "one should not underrate the cultural efficiency of a tenacious adherence to archaic institutions in the face of any eventuality" [1915, 237].

CHAPTER 5

SOCIAL EVOLUTION

The primary force driving social evolution is technological change. New technologies disrupt old habits and patterns of behavior. The result is a new set of habits and institutions. As Veblen put it, "social evolution is a process of selective adaptation of temperament and habits of thought under the stress of the circumstances of associated life. The adaptation of habits of thought is the growth of institutions" [1899, 213]. The process has no endpoint because technology, the environment and institutions will continue to change.

Social evolution is relentless, even if at times it is quite slow due to institutional rigidity. Ultimately, it is the product of human nature itself. Humans, by virtue of being human, will act, and that action will unwittingly change the societies in which they live. In a well-known passage Veblen wrote that

> The growth of culture is a cumulative sequence of habituation, and the ways and means of it are the habitual response of human nature to exigencies that vary incontinently, cumulatively, but with something

of a consistent sequence in the cumulative variations that so go forward,--incontinently, because each new moves creates a new situation which induces a further new variation in the habitual manner of response; cumulatively, because each new situation is a variation of what has gone before it and embodies as causal factors all that has been effected by what went before; consistently, because the underlying traits of human nature (propensities, aptitudes, and what not) by force of which response takes place, and on the ground of which habituation takes effect, remain substantially unchanged [1919, 241-2].

The future evolution of a society cannot be predicted. All Darwinian evolutionary processes are non-teleological. But archaeology and history provide clues to how society evolved in the past. Veblen, influenced by the work of Lewis Henry Morgan and a few other anthropologists, divided past social evolution into four broad stages [Edgell, 2001, 88].

The oldest stage lasted until the early Neolithic period. Veblen dubbed this period one of "savagery," though its culture was "of a relatively advanced kind as compared with the rudest human beginnings" [1914, 118]. Contrary to what many others have assumed about this era, Veblen argued that it was "fairly peaceable" [Ibid. 120]. The low level of technology of the time required everyone to spend their time making a living. Besides, other groups did not have anything worth stealing. In this period, a community "can not afford to be habitually occupied with annoying its neighbours, particularly so long as its neighbours have not accumulated a store of portable wealth which will make raiding worth while" [Ibid. 123]. Veblen bolsters his case by reporting that archaeologists had recovered relatively few weapons and a large number of tools from the period.

The peaceable nature of the period gave free reign to the instincts of parental bent and workmanship. Groups that emphasized predatory instincts could not survive. Technological change was very slow, as there was very little time for idle curiosity. But over the long period of time that the era occupied, change did occur. There was improvement in many areas, including tool making, woodworking and agriculture.

The cumulative effect of even slow technological change is an increase in industrial efficiency. Overtime, societies that had been living on the edge of subsistence improved their technology enough to generate an economic surplus, that is, "an accumulation of wealth beyond the current necessities of subsistence" [Ibid. 150]. The surplus led to profound changes in the institutional structure. Veblen dubbed the new evolutionary stage the predatory or barbarian culture.

A surplus gives scope to the self-regarding instincts. If there is a surplus, it becomes possible for some to survive without contributing to production. As a result, predatory individuals seek to gain control over the surplus and the means to produce it. Veblen contended that the two primary channels of control were religion and warfare. Shamans or medicine men live "half parasitically, by some sort of tithe levied on their fellow members for supernatural ministrations" [Ibid. 155]. In other words, shamans extracted payments for "supernatural" services that did not contribute to the material well being of the community. Members of the group exempted from work because of the surplus are also free to make war on other groups. The wealth that accumulates because of the surplus is "an inducement to aggression" [Ibid. 156]. War chiefs arise to lead raids. In his typical wry style, Veblen wrote that

> Given a sufficiently wealthy enemy who is suffi-
> ciently ill prepared for hostilities to afford a fighting
> chance of taking over this wealth by way of booty
> or tribute, with no obvious chance of due reprisals,
> and the opening of hostilities will commonly arrange
> itself [Ibid. 156-7].

Over time, the formerly peaceable community develops "a more or less habitual attitude of predatory exploit" [Ibid. 157].

Predatory habits help develop the institution of ownership. In the period of savagery, property rights were non-existent or ill defined, partly because there was so little to own aside from personal trinkets and partly because of the dominance of group-regarding habits. In the predatory culture, self-regarding instincts come to the fore and the pool of wealth is greater. Loot from a raid may be claimed by the one who took it. The loot may take the form of goods, tools, land or people. Conventions arise regarding ownership of the trophies of war. Individuals are granted exclusive use of the things and people they take in war. Over time, habituation to the idea of ownership ex-tends property rights to similar items controlled or produced by the group itself. Warfare and religion, which Veblen dubbed "force" and "fraud" [Ibid. 159], brought about the institution of private property that is still central to the modern economy.

The instinct of workmanship comes to be directed by the self-regarding motives that govern the period. An obvious application of workmanship is the production of weapons and of religious para-phernalia and monuments. As time progressed, the institution of ownership itself became honorable because it was associated with high-status war chiefs and religious leaders. In other words, everyone with status also had a significant amount of property, so property itself was evidence of status. If there were no opportunities to acquire wealth through war or religion, people came to seek wealth through work. Nevertheless, the instinct of workmanship was often suppressed because work was associated with the slaves taken in raids. Moreover, high-status individuals were sufficiently wealthy to not have to work. Consequently, "work becomes a mark of inferiority and is therefore discreditable" [Ibid. 174].

Veblen locates the "higher stages of the barbarian culture" in feudal Europe and feudal Japan [1899, 1]. The upper classes in these places were exempt from any form of manual labor or business. Such occupations were deemed beneath them. The elite devoted their attention exclusively to warfare and religion.

Even in the modern era, an exemption from useful work is a mark of status. The implications are profound, and will be explored in a later chapter. But it is worthwhile to examine this pervasive habit of thought in more detail. As already mentioned, its origin is the association of work with slaves taken in raids. The first slaves were probably women. Drudgery came to be associated with women, and no self-respecting male could be caught doing "women's work." Men sought employments that have some element of exploit, such as war, hunting or religion. In the modern era, "a distinction is still habitually made between industrial and non-industrial occupations; and this modern distinction is a transmuted form of the barbarian distinction between exploit and drudgery" [Veblen, 1899, 9-10]. Industrial occupations have to do with making useful goods or providing useful services. Non-industrial occupations have to do with control of other people or of property. It is a peculiar inversion of thinking that causes us to award higher status to lawyers than to farmers, even though farmers provide us with the most important goods we buy. Think about that. The people who produce life's necessities generally have very little status. The reason is that for a large part of human history, the people who performed such "drudgery" were owned or controlled by others. The habit of thought associating such occupations with low status persists to this day. Veblen delineated a hierarchy of employment according to status:

> Employments fall into a hierarchical gradation of reputability. Those which have to do immediately with ownership on a large scale are the most reputable of economic employments proper. Next to these in good repute come those that are immediately subservient to ownership and financiering, -- such as banking and the law. Banking employments also carry a suggestion of large ownership, and this fact is doubtless accountable for a share of the prestige that attaches to the business. The profession of the law does not imply large ownership; but since no taint of usefulness, for other than competitive purpose, attaches to the lawyer's trade, it grades high in the conventional scheme. The lawyer is exclusively occupied with the details of predatory fraud, either in achieving or in checkmating chicane, and success in the profession is therefore accepted as marking a large endowment of that barbarian astuteness which has always commanded men's respect and fear. Mercantile pursuits are only half-way reputable, unless they involve a large element of ownership and a small element of

usefulness ... Manual labour, or even the work of
directing mechanical processes, is of course on a pre-
carious footing as regards respectability [Ibid. 232]

Many more people aspire to be bankers than plumbers, even though
plumbers are certainly more necessary to our health and comfort.

Despite the fact that the barbarian era encouraged an aversion to
productive labor, we never would have reached the modern era if
large numbers of people had not worked diligently. The pendulum
began to swing back in the direction of work as a reputable activity
during the later stages of the predatory culture. Over time, ownership became a legitimate end in itself. It became just another means
of self-aggrandizement, and status could be obtained simply by being rich. Success in blatantly predatory activities was still the "best"
way to acquire wealth, but work was an increasingly acceptable
method too. A class of people emerged who acquired property primarily through work or business, not war or religion. This "middle"
class had status because it had property. The negative image of work
had not disappeared, but "so long as work is of a visibly pecuniary
kind and is sagaciously and visibly directed to the acquisition of
wealth, the disrepute intrinsically attaching to it is greatly offset by
its meritorious purpose" [Ibid. 183-4]. In other words, if one can
acquire wealth by shrewd trading, then one's predatory credentials
are intact. The wealth acquired is a form of trophy that provides
evidence of one's business prowess.

As the practice of acquiring wealth in this fashion became more
widespread, the values and habits of thought of the middle class
gained force. War destroys the hard-won gains of the class, and so
gradually sentiment shifted against the overtly predatory behavior

common in feudal Europe. The transition from a purely predatory culture to a commercial culture signified "the emergence of a middle class in such force as presently to recast the working arrangements of the cultural scheme and make peaceable business the ruling interest of the community" [Ibid. 184-5].

The gradual rise of the middle class marks a transition to what Veblen called the handicraft era. It is characterized by a significant number of independent craftsmen and businessmen. Veblen described it as peaceable or quasi-peaceable because the middle class did not have an interest in the more or less constant warfare that plagued Europe. The growing size and influence of the middle class acted to reduce, though certainly not stop, the frequency of war. That, in turn, made property more secure. Secure property provided an incentive to work harder, which increased productivity. It also created an intellectual climate that was more favorable to technological change. The business class had a direct interest in increasing the efficiency of industry because lower costs meant higher profits.

As noted above, Veblen drew a distinction between "business" and "industry." Business has to do with making money. Industry has to do with making goods. As will be discussed in more detail later, business and industry are related, but they are not the same thing. The ultimate objective of business is to gain wealth so as to gain status. In that regard it is part of the predatory culture [Ibid. 216]. The objective of industry is to produce things that other people want. It is in keeping with the group-regarding instincts. Veblen makes it clear that the emerging middle class was primarily interested in business, not industry. Industry was just a means to an end in that it produced the goods that were traded. During this time, improvements in industry typically led to improvements in business, so new technologies were encouraged.

The instinct of workmanship flourished during the handicraft era. This instinctive tendency in human nature was encouraged by the institution of ownership and the commercial culture that measured success in terms of accumulated wealth. The ethic of hard work and frugality gained acceptance as a means to accumulate wealth. Diligent application of the instinct of workmanship was an alternative to war and religion in the quest for status.

The growing economic surplus meant that more people could indulge their instinctive idle curiosity. As already mentioned, idle curiosity is the fundamental source of new knowledge and ideas. The new ideas generated provided the raw material that the instinct of workmanship turned into useful applications. The pace of technological change quickened.

Improvements in technology eventually changed the nature of the economic system. Masterless craftsmen, working in guilds or independently, characterized the handicraft era. The tools required were typically simple enough for most workers to own, or even to make. But as technology improved, the equipment needed to make use of it became increasingly sophisticated and expensive. It was also extensive enough to require more than one worker to use it. Only the wealthier craftsmen could afford the equipment, and they needed others to help them use it. To solve this problem they hired others to work with them, and increasingly, for them. "So capitalism emerged from the working of the handicraft system, through the increasing scale and efficiency of technology" [Veblen, Ibid. 282].

Veblen argued that the system commonly called capitalism is, "from the point of view of technology, ... best characterised as the era of the machine industry, or of the machine process" [Ibid. 299]. The machine era overlaps the handicraft era considerably, and elements of the handicraft era remain to this day. But the present era is dominated by large-scale, machine-using enterprises.

The era of machine industry brought with it not just greater industrial efficiency but also major changes in habits of thought and patterns of living. In a previous chapter it was mentioned that workers no longer worked at home, and became subject to the discipline of the clock. But the effects of machine industry reached even deeper. Mechanical processes "are calculable, measurable, and contain no mysterious element of providential ambiguity" [Ibid. 306]. They encourage matter-of-fact, "scientific" thinking. Habits of thought developed by machine industry suppress superstition and anthropomorphism. Economies dominated by agriculture are subject to the whims of nature. It is easy to attribute natural forces to supernatural beings because they can seem capricious and are out of one's control. Economies dominated by machines leave less room for the metaphysical. As Veblen wrote,

> With due but not large exceptions, the effective body of the modern population has been growing more matter-of-fact in their thinking, less romantic, less idealistic in their aspirations, less bound by metaphysical considerations in their view of human relations, less mannerly, less devout [1904, 345].

Veblen's observation still applies. Church attendance has collapsed in Europe, though it is still strong in the United States. And in both places, commentators routinely note the lack of civility and manners that permeates society.

Science and practical technology became linked as never before. The central thesis of Mokyr's [2002] celebrated book is that the roots of the industrial revolution can be found in an "industrial enlightenment" that preceded it. Veblen made essentially the same point a century earlier. It is the advancement in knowledge that drives all such changes. The change was dramatic because of the explosion in knowledge. Knowledge has continued to grow rapidly because the machine process itself encourages scientific thinking. Science is not new, but a systematic, machine-like "pursuit of impersonal relations of causal sequence" [Veblen, 1904, 361] is.

> The beginnings of modern science are older than the industrial revolution; the principles of scientific research (causal explanation and exact measurement) antedate the regime of the machine process. But a change has taken place in the postulates and animus of scientific research since modern science first began, and this change in the postulates of scientific knowledge is related to the growth of the machine technology [Ibid. 363].

The advance in technology required that workers be more literate and better schooled. The need for more educated workers even led Veblen to suggest that laws limiting child labor had an economic as well as a humanitarian motive [1914, 309]. Whatever the motive, more widespread education benefited science as well as industry. Scientific advances led to fresh advances in useful technology.

It is worth noting that the machine era requires more workers who are literate, but fewer with the very specialized skills of the craftsman. Veblen wrote that

> The special training required for service as opera-
> tive workmen in the common run of the machine
> industries is very greatly less than the corresponding
> workman under the handicraft system. General in-
> formation and manual dexterity, together with some,
> relatively slight, special habituation to the particular
> processes involved in the given mechanical occu-
> pation, is all that is needed in this way to make a
> very passable working force in the machine industry
> [1915, 188].

Mass education meets the requirements without the need for the lengthy apprenticeships of the handicraft era.

Resistance to new technology is always present. Many of the Luddite riots (1811-1816) and the Captain Swing riots (1830-1832) in England were direct responses to the introduction of new technology [Mokyr, 2002, 267]. Workers, and in the case of the Captain Swing riots some of the landed gentry, objected to new methods that threatened their livelihoods and traditional relationships. But business interests had much to gain, so the riots were brutally suppressed. In 1813, fourteen Luddites were hung [Easterly, 2002, 53]. The commercial culture was by that time quite strong, and in such a culture, "invention is the mother of necessity" [Veblen, 1914, 314]. That means that competitive pressure forces businesses to adopt any new invention that improves business. They really have no choice. "Any technological advantage gained by one competitor forthwith becomes a necessity to all the rest, on pain of defeat" [Ibid. 315]. Any new technology that improves profits will be adopted. If a firm fails to do so, its competitors will drive it out of business.

At a broader level, Veblen discussed how the era of the machine makes the overall pattern of life more machine-like. Life is scheduled and standardized. Large-scale industry requires large numbers of workers who must arrive at work at the same time. The clock governs when we get up, when we work, when we eat and when we sleep. Personal biological rhythms must be suppressed if one is to function in the machine era. Human nature has not evolved to make the adjustment easy. "Neither the manner of life imposed by the machine process, nor the manner of thought inculcated by habituation to its logic, will fall in with the free movement of the human spirit, born, as it is, to fit the conditions of savage life" [Veblen, Ibid. 334].

Forcing ourselves to live by the discipline of the machine era takes a toll on our health and sanity. Not only are we regimented by our work schedule, but we also find it hard to relax outside of work. Use of devices that speed communication, such as the telephone, "involves a very appreciable nervous strain and its ubiquitous presence conduces to an unremitting nervous tension and unrest" [Veblen, Ibid. 316]. Keep in mind that Veblen was writing long before cell phones came to intrude upon every waking minute. And hard as it may be for us to imagine, the telegraph had a similar effect. In 1868 a New York businessman complained that "the businessman of the present day must be continually on the jump - he must use the telegraph" [Economist, 2005b, 58].

The result is an "increase in nervous disorders and shortening of the effective working life" [Ibid. 316]. We dream of a return to Nature, to the "simple life" which we think will "afford an escape from the unending 'grind' of living from day to day by the machine method"

[Ibid. 319]. Veblen noted how the custom of "taking a vacation" was on the increase. He wrote that

> This growing recourse to vacations should be pass-ably conclusive evidence to the effect that neither the manner of life enforced by the machine system, nor the occupations of those who are in close contact with this technology and its due habits of thought, can be "natural" to the common run of civilised man-kind [Ibid. 319-20].

No careful observer of life in the twenty-first century can fail to see the prophetic nature of Veblen's pronouncement.

Business is the central institution in the machine era. For that reason Veblen examined it in some detail. We will explore his thoughts on it in a subsequent chapter.

CHAPTER 6

THE LAST TRAIN
RUNS THE FASTEST

There are two ways by which a society can acquire a new technology. It can develop it itself, or it can borrow it from another society. Veblen argued that borrowing technology has advantages that go far beyond the fact that the borrower does not have to pay to develop the technology.

As already noted, a new technology will eventually cause new institutions to develop that will restrict its use. For example, habits of thought may arise that allow only certain members of the society to use the technology, and only at certain times and for certain purposes. In earlier eras, the constraints often took the form of superstitions. Veblen gave the example of the Aleutian Islanders "slushing about in the wrack and surf with rakes and magical incantations for the capture of shell-fish" [1919, 193]. Such "naive forms of mandatory futility" [1915, 27] limit the usefulness of any technology. The Aleutian Islanders could have harvested more shell-fish if they did not have to wait for a shaman's presence, and if some of the group's labor was not devoted to casting incantations.

In modern times, the constraining institutions tend to be more secular, but the effect is the same. As will be discussed in more detail later, the institution called business largely controls how we use our industrial technology. During a recession, society suffers a loss of output not because it is unable to produce, but because business does not allow it to produce. Business habits of thought can limit the use of technology just as surely as superstition. The belief in magical incantations and the logic of business are both institutions that can restrict production. In a similar vein, every modern organization, public or private, is forced to devote labor to insure that a long list of rules and regulations imposed by the legal system are enforced, even though many of the rules are of dubious value. Highly paid administrators and managers are employed to oversee rules that in no way further the objectives of the organization, and sometimes even cause it harm. Nobody likes "bureaucracy," and it is widely condemned because it is seen as a waste of labor. Bureaucracy nevertheless permeates our society.

The longer a technology has been with a society, the more institutional constraints may develop on its use. In the United States, one need only think of the thicket of new laws that eventually crop up around every new technology. Regulation of the Internet has already begun. Over time, the use of a technology can become severely circumscribed by institutions.

If another society borrows a technology, it will generally do so "from motives of workmanlike expediency" [Veblen, 1914, 136]. In other words, it borrows the technology because it sees its usefulness.

As a rule, it will not borrow the institutions that reduce the value of the technology. The technology will therefore have wider scope in the borrowing society than in the inventing society. Over time, institutions restricting the use of the technology will emerge in the borrowing society, but for a while, the technology will face fewer "institutional inhibitions" [Veblen, 1915, 28].

Without institutional constraints, the borrowing society is in a better position than the inventing society to make full use of the borrowed technologies. In addition, the borrowing society has "a better chance of improving on their use [and] turning them to new uses" [Ibid. 38]. In other words, without restrictive laws and habits of thought, the new users of the technologies are freer to apply and extend them as they see fit. This allows for the possibility that the borrowing society will develop the technologies to a higher level than the inventing society. The student can surpass the teacher.

A second advantage for a borrowing society is that it has no investment in older versions of the technology. This is especially important for infrastructure. Veblen gives the example of the British railway system which was "built with too narrow a gauge" [Ibid. 130]. Great Britain was the first country to build an extensive railway system. As a result, it built "terminal facilities, tracks, shunting facilities, and all the ways and means of handling freight" [Ibid.] in accordance with early railroad technology. As the technology advanced, it became apparent in hindsight that all of these things would be more useful if they had been built differently, in accordance with the more modern technology. But it is not an easy thing to scrap an entire railroad system and replace it with a new one. Great Britain was stuck with an antiquated railway system. That exemplifies the penalty for taking the lead.

The position of a country without a railroad system is much different. It can borrow the latest railroad technology and build a system according to the new technology. The railroad system of the borrowing country would then be superior to the system in Great Britain. Great Britain did all the work to develop railroads, but wound up with an inferior railroad system. Moreover, the longer a country waits to build its railroad system, the better the railroad technology it borrows will be. That is why the last train runs the fastest.

PART III
CAPITAL AND
BUSINESS ENTERPRISE

Veblen viewed all eras as transient. Social evolution is continuous, as is the technological change that is its main catalyst. In fact, labeling a time period as an era is itself artificial. Evolution operates at all times. Society changes within each era and the eras themselves overlap considerably. Naming an era was primarily a way of recognizing that certain general tendencies dominated roughly defined time periods.

The era in which Veblen was writing was, by historical measures, quite young. He knew that it would continue to evolve and change. Nevertheless, there was no doubt about what the dominant institutions were: ownership, business enterprise and "an habitual and conventionally righteous disregard of other than pecuniary considerations" [Veblen, 1914, 347]. Status was measured in pecuniary (monetary) terms, and competition for a place in the social hierarchy was carried out on that basis.

Ownership of large amounts of capital gives one control over business enterprise. It also makes one wealthy, automatically conferring high status. The ownership of capital is so central that it is worth examining Veblen's view of it in some detail.

CHAPTER 7

CAPITAL

The word capital as it is used in economics has more than one meaning. A leading principles of economics textbook defines capital as "the equipment and structures used to produce goods and services" [Mankiw, 2004, 829]. The same book discusses the phenomenon of "capital flight." Capital flight from, say, Mexico, means that investors "decide to sell some of their Mexican assets and use the proceeds to buy U.S. assets" [Ibid. 712]. The "capital" that is in flight from Mexico is not the "capital" defined as equipment and structures; Mexican machines and buildings are not migrating north. The "capital" leaving Mexico is a sum of money; it is, in Veblen's phrase, a "pecuniary entity."

The source of the confusion can be traced back to John Bates Clark, who originated modern neoclassical capital theory (and was one of Veblen's teachers). Clark drew a distinction between "capital goods," which are equipment and structures, and "capital," which is a fund of value. Capital as a fund has value because it represents ownership of capital goods. Over time, particular capital goods wear out and are replaced, but capital remains [Clark, 1899, 116-40].

Clark drew the distinction between capital goods and capital because he wanted to argue two things. The first is that the income that goes to owners of capital is a result of the contribution to output made by the equipment and buildings they own. In other words, the income given to owners of capital goods comes out of the extra output produced with the use of their capital goods. The idea, called marginal productivity theory, is now part of neoclassical dogma, and can be found in most every textbook[6]. The second point Clark wanted to make is that capital can flow from one industry to another. Capital goods tend to be industry specific, and cannot easily change industries. The capital goods used in the automobile industry cannot be used to make textiles. So how can capital be mobile if it represents ownership of capital goods? According to Clark, it is able to do so because the capital goods in the automobile industry generate income as they wear out. The income generated can be used to buy capital goods in the textile industry. In that fashion, the value of capital in the automobile industry shrinks and it rises in the textile industry.

As capital moves into an industry, the quantity of capital goods in the industry rises. The additional capital goods allow for additional production. For this reason, neoclassical theory argues that capital is "productive." Its productivity gives it value. The same argument can be applied to labor, land, or anything else that contributes to production. Adding more labor or land generally increases output, so labor and land are said to be productive.

Veblen rejected Clark's analysis for several reasons. Veblen accused neoclassical economics of being "taxonomic," that is, more concerned with establishing a system of classification for economic activity than of actually analyzing economic activity. Clark was concerned about classifying the contribution to production made by capital, labor, and land. He attributed the return to each of these resources to their marginal products. To Veblen, an obsession with neat systems of classification made neoclassical economists overlook an obvious point: production is a social process, and the "productivity" of any resource ultimately stems from the society's technology. One cannot isolate the contribution of any one resource and pretend it is some-how distinct from the knowledge of how to use it. Capital goods, for example, are not inherently productive; they simply embody tech-nology and are the means to use that technology. A sophisticated machine in the midst of a stone-age tribe is not productive. Veblen wrote that

> all tangible assets owe their productivity and their value to the immaterial industrial expedients which they embody ... . Those immaterial industrial expedi-ents are necessarily a product of the community, the immaterial residue of the community's experience, past and present; which has no existence apart from the community's life, and can be transmitted only in the keeping of the community at large ... . What there is involved in the material equipment, which is not of this immaterial, spiritual nature, and so what is not an immaterial residue of the community's experience, is the raw material out of which the industrial appli-ances are constructed, with the stress falling wholly on the "raw" [1919, 347-8].

The same idea applies to labor:

> As workman, labourer, producer, breadwinner, the
> individual is a creature of the technological scheme;
> which in turn is a creation of the group life of the
> community. Apart from the common stock of knowl-
> edge and training the individual members of the
> community have no industrial effect [1914, 144-5].

As already discussed, a community's technology is possessed and
transmitted by the group. Virtually everything a worker knows is
drawn from that stock of communal knowledge. Raw labor has no
economic value. Capital goods have value only because we know
how to use them. In fact, all economic resources become economic
resources only when we figure out how to use them. Metal ores had
no value until we discovered how to transform them into useful objects. Oil became valuable only after we found out how to use it.
As noted in an earlier chapter, a society's technology is its most
valuable possession.

Veblen argued that neoclassical economists did not count technology as a productive factor like capital, labor and land because it
doesn't receive a payment such as profit, wages or rent [1921, 27-8].
Economists and others have made the mistake of assuming that anything "productive" receives a payment. But profit, wages and rent
are paid only because there are property rights over capital goods,
labor and land, and because these resources are scarce. Technology
is possessed by the group, so no individual or group receives a payment for it. The exception proves the rule: in the case of a patent,
where a specific piece of knowledge is owned, a payment is made
to the owner for its use. In the pursuit of convenient taxonomies,

property rights have been confused with productivity.

If technology is the source of capital goods' "productivity," and if technology is possessed by society as a whole, how did it come about that owners of capital goods could demand payment for their use? Veblen argued that capital goods did not always generate income, but came to do so as technology improved. In societies with simple technology, the material equipment needed to use the technology was also simple. Ownership of the necessary tools was not of much consequence because they could easily be obtained by anyone who wanted them. Veblen guessed that this was the case for 90 percent of human history [1919, 330]. But as technology advanced, the material equipment needed to use it became more sophisticated and difficult to acquire. Over time, fewer and fewer people could afford to own it. The people who could afford to own capital goods found themselves in the position of deciding the terms on which society could use its technology. In other words, technology was still possessed by the community as a whole, but the means to use it was in the hands of a relative few. The advantage this gave to the owners of capital goods was very similar to the advantage enjoyed by owners of land. Like capital goods, not everyone can afford to own land, and land is also necessary to employ technology. As a result, owners of land can decide the terms on which it can be used. Veblen described how the "unearned increment" known as land rent exists solely because of the state of technology and the legal position of landowners:

> The unearned increment, it is held, is produced by the growth of the community in numbers and in the industrial arts. The contention seems to be sound, and is commonly accepted; but it has commonly been

overlooked that the argument involves the ulterior conclusion that all land values and land productivity, including the "original and indestructible powers of the soil," are a function of the "state of the industrial art." It is only within the given technological situation, the current scheme of ways and means, that any parcel of land has such productive powers as it has. It is, in other words, useful only because, and in so far, and in such manner, as men have learned to make use of it. This is what brings it into the category of "land," economically speaking. And the preferential position of the landlord as a claimant of the "net product" consists in his legal right to decide whether, how far, and on what terms men shall put this technological scheme into effect in those features of it which involve the use of his parcel of land [Ibid. 337-8].

Veblen immediately added that "all this argument concerning the unearned increment may be carried over, with scarcely a change of phrase, to the case of 'capital goods'" [Ibid. 338]. Owning capital goods gives one the legal right to "decide whether, how far, and on what terms" society can make use of its technology. Like land, capital goods generate income not because they are productive but because they are scarce. If capital goods were less scarce, they would be less valuable but not less productive.[7] Nevertheless, "for practical purposes, the advanced 'state of the industrial arts' has enabled the owners of goods to corner the wisdom of the ancients and the accumulated experience of the race" [Ibid. 186]. Society's ability to use its technology is held hostage by the owners of capital goods.

The legal ability to extract a payment from society for the right to use its technology makes ownership of capital goods attractive. That leads to the practice of investment in capital. Both investment and capital are pecuniary entities; they are measured in terms of money. At first glance, Veblen and Clark seem to be in agreement on this point. But Veblen disputes Clark's contention that the value of capital is simply the value of the capital goods associated with the capital.

For Veblen, ownership of capital implies ownership of two types of assets. The first, tangible assets, consists of the material equipment used in production, and corresponds to Clark's capital goods. The second, intangible assets, consists of all the immaterial things that affect the value of a given block of capital. Intangible assets include things like brand names, trademarks, "good will," patents, and legal privileges granted to the firm. Such assets give a firm a differential advantage over competitors, and enhance its earning capacity. They also have no place in Clark's scheme [Ibid. 220].

People want to own capital because it will generate income. The value of a given amount of capital is therefore determined by the present value of the expected stream of income it will generate. As Veblen put it, "'Capital' means 'capitalized putative earning capacity'" [1904, 131]. Both types of assets contribute to earning capacity. Tangible assets contribute to the value of capital in that they "capitalise such fraction of the technological proficiency of the community as the ownership of the capital goods involved enables the owner to engross" [Veblen, 1919, 365]. Intangible assets contribute to the value of capital because they "capitalise such habits of life, of a non-technological character,--settled by usage, convention, arrogation, legislative action, or what not,--as will effect a differential advantage to the concern to which the assets in question appertain" [Ibid. 365].

In other words, the value of things like trademarks, which have no effect on productivity, are capitalized and are reflected in the value of a firm's capital. To put it simply, tangible assets have to do with technology; intangible assets have to do with institutions. Capital is more than just a collection of capital goods.

A famous brand name is valuable because it affects the firm's earning capacity. Because it affects earning capacity, the value of the brand name is reflected in the value of the firm's capital. Veblen drives the point home by pointing out that firms expend real resources to create a valuable brand name. In so doing, they convert tangible assets into intangible assets. That is the rationale for advertising. Real resources are used to improve the firm's reputation. By so doing, the firm will enjoy a larger stream of income, which will increase the value of its capital. An improved reputation allows it to sell more output, which means that the intangible asset ultimately leads to more tangible assets in the form of finished products. Veblen wrote that

> To any one preoccupied with the conceit that "capital" means "capital goods" such a conversion of intangible into tangible goods, or such a generation of intangible assets by the productive use of tangible assets, might be something of a puzzle. If "assets" were a physical concept, covering a range of physical things, instead of a pecuniary concept, such conversion of tangible into intangible assets, and conversely, would be a case of transubstantiation [Ibid. 370].

Advertising is not the only thing that can affect the value of capital. A technological change can make a firm's product or method of production obsolete. The value of its capital will collapse, even though the firm's equipment is no less productive than it was before the new technology appeared. Typewriter companies saw the value of their capital plummet after personal computers were introduced, even though their typewriter manufacturing equipment still worked. Or consider the case of monopoly. A monopoly can increase profits (and the value of its capital) by reducing production. Likewise, during a recession, firms will cease production rather than operate at a loss. In other words, protecting the value of capital requires that capital goods not be used. The productive use of capital goods can reduce the value of capital, so owners of capital goods choose at times not to use them. Obviously, the neoclassical idea that the value of capital is tightly linked to its productivity is flawed.

The behavior of firms during a recession or in a monopoly position illustrates a broader point. Business interests and community interests do not always coincide. Business controls industry, and whether industry operates at its potential is a business decision. As Veblen observed, "Pecuniary ... advantage to the capitalist-manager has, under the regime of investment, taken precedence of economic advantage to the community: or rather, the differential advantage of ownership is alone regarded in the conduct of industry under this system" [Ibid. 355]. Even if large segments of the population experience economic hardship, the community can be denied use of its technology. Business, as the dominant institution in the machine era, decides how, when and if production takes place. Business decisions are made with reference to pecuniary concerns alone. Nothing else matters to business. As Veblen wrote,

> The material necessities of a group of workmen or
> consumers ... is, therefore, not competent to set aside,
> or indeed to qualify, the natural freedom of the own-
> ers of these processes to let work go on or not, as the
> outlook for profits may decide. Profits is a business
> proposition, livelihood is not [1904, 276].

Business limits output to the amount that is profitable to produce.
It does not produce all that industry is capable of producing, nor
does it produce all that the population might need. Veblen calls this
restriction of output a "conscientious withdrawal of efficiency"
[1921, 1], and then labels it as "sabotage."

The ability to sabotage production stems from the institution of
ownership. The legal title to capital goods, like the ownership of
land, puts the owner in the position of dictating the terms on which
society can use its technology. The method of enforcing the terms
is the threat of not allowing production to take place. As Veblen
put it,

> By virtue of this legal right of sabotage which inheres
> as a natural right in the ownership of industrially
> useful things, the owners are able to dictate satisfac-
> tory terms; so that they come in for the usufruct of
> the community's industrial knowledge and practice,
> with such deductions as are necessary to enforce
> their terms and such concessions as will induce the
> underlying population to go on with the work. This
> making of terms is called "Charging what the traffic
> will bear" [1923, 67].

In other words, the decision as to what resources will be used, and
if they will be used, lies with the owner. If the owner does not re-

ceive sufficient compensation, the resources will not be used and society will not be able to use its technology. Veblen argued that the enormous productive capacity of modern industry would never be used to its fullest because the glut of goods produced would depress prices and therefore profit. Some amount of unemployment, therefore, would become the typical state of affairs [Ibid. 112].

Sabotage is also practiced by labor unions when they strike or have a slowdown. After all, labor is necessary to use technology. But it is business that primarily determines whether production takes place or not. It is important, therefore, to examine the institution of business in more detail.

CHAPTER 8

BUSINESS ENTERPRISE AND THE INDUSTRIAL SYSTEM

Economic activity takes place in a wide range of circumstances, including at home. But the heart of what is generally called "the economy" is the industrial system under the control of business. The two main features of the modern economy are "the machine process and investment for profit" [Veblen, 1904, 1].

To Veblen, "the machine process" means more than just the use of machines. He defines it as "a reasoned procedure on the basis of a systematic knowledge of the forces employed" [Ibid. 6]. In other words, it is the application of science and engineering to production. Even modern agriculture is part of the machine process because it employs "a determinate, reasoned routine" in place of "the rule of thumb" [Ibid. 7n]. Moreover, the industrial system as a whole can be considered a machine process. Industries do not operate in isolation. An industry will buy what it needs from other industries and sell what it produces to still other industries. Individual firms all operate as part of "a comprehensive, balanced mechanical process" [Ibid. 16]. The different parts of the industrial system depend on each other and work together in a manner not unlike a giant machine.

The smooth functioning of the industrial system requires two things: "(a) the running maintenance of interstitial adjustments between the several sub-processes or branches of industry ... ; and (b) an unremitting requirement of quantitative precision" [Ibid. 8].

"The running maintenance of interstitial adjustments" means that there must be a continuous coordination of all the firms involved in the system. To keep the machine running smoothly, firms must receive the right inputs in the right quantities and at the right times. A failure to do so will not only bring the firms directly affected to a halt, but will also adversely affect firms further down the supply chain. A breakdown at any point in the system can wreak havoc on large parts of the economy. The critical task of coordination is accomplished through business transactions. It follows, therefore, that any business disturbance soon becomes an industrial disturbance.

"An unremitting requirement of quantitative precision" means that most inputs must be standardized with respect to "weight, size, density, hardness, tensile strength, elasticity, temperature, chemical reaction, actinic sensitiveness, etc." [Ibid. 8]. Any bolt chosen at random must be able to fit any nut of the same size. There is no need to custom-make each part individually as was the case in the handicraft era. As a result, craftsman-like skills are no longer required for routine work. If one's car requires a part, one can buy it off the shelf; there is no need to have one custom-made. Standardization saves an enormous amount of skilled labor.

As already mentioned, industry and the machine process are under the control of business. The objective of business is to make money. That means that the economic welfare of the society is secondary to the goal of profit. If throwing sand on the gears of the machine process will make businessmen[8] money, then they will throw sand. As Veblen wrote,

> The economic welfare of the community at large is best served by a facile and uninterrupted interplay of the various processes which make up the industrial system at large; but the pecuniary interests of the business men in whose hands lies discretion in the matter are not necessarily best served by an unbroken maintenance of the industrial balance [Ibid. 27].

The most obvious example occurs during a recession or depression. From a purely industrial point of view, the ability to produce the things the community wants is unaffected. From a business standpoint, output must be reduced in order to avoid losing money. Because business controls industry, the business perspective wins out. The irony is that in previous eras, economic hardship was due to an inability to produce, caused by bad weather or war. The result was high prices for necessities. In the modern era, hardship is caused by low prices that make it unprofitable to produce [Ibid. 177].

Veblen traces the origin of the typical depression to the interplay of capital values and loan credit. As mentioned previously, the value of capital is ultimately governed by the present value of expected future profit. Ownership of capital is motivated by a desire to earn a monetary return. The desirability of any particular block of capital therefore depends on the income it is expected to generate. The problem is that the future is by definition uncertain. The precise amount of future revenues and costs are unknowable. As a result, capital values ultimately depend on the optimism or pessimism of investors. In other words, "the magnitude of the business capital and its mutations from day to day are in great measure a question of folk psychology rather than material fact" [Ibid. 149].[9] The value of capital rests on nothing solid, and certainly does not depend on the physical productivity of tangible assets alone.

Veblen described how a business cycle might occur. Consider an economy operating below its productive capacity. Then suppose there is an increase in demand for the output of a few industries, such as occurred when the demand for war materiel increased at the outbreak of the Spanish-American War [Ibid. 194]. The immediate effect is an increase in the prices of the industries' output. The firms affected respond by increasing production. To do so, they increase their demand for the supplies that they need. They may also purchase new equipment. The new investment is fueled by the firms' increased earnings, which increases the value of their capital. The increase in demand for supplies and for equipment raises demand in more remote parts of the economy as the suppliers demand more from their suppliers, and so on. The result is a general increase in prices throughout the economy.

The increase in prices leads to an increase in earnings. In addition, the general prosperity leads to a "lively anticipation" [Ibid. 195] of further increases in demand and consequently an anticipation of higher future earnings. As a result, "extensive contracts for future performance are entered into in all directions, and this extensive implication of the various lines of industry serves, of itself, to maintain the prosperity for the time being" [Ibid. 195-6]. Veblen argued that there is a "habit of buoyancy, or speculative reckless-ness, which grows up in any business community under such cir-cumstances" [Ibid. 196]. One need only consider the recent "dot. com" bubble to see that speculative recklessness (or Fed Chairman Greenspan's "irrational exuberance") is still with us.

The rise in earnings and anticipated earnings increases capital values. Owning capital is especially attractive when it is increas-ing in value, so the demand for it rises. The increase in demand is fueled by credit. Lenders are eager to lend in good times [Ibid. 190]. The inflow of credit drives up stock prices, which are the most immediate measure of the value of capital. Capital is used as collateral for loans, so a rise in its value allows for a further exten-sion of credit. The additional credit is used to buy more capital, and so on. The cycle will continue, helped along by the aforemen-tioned "speculative recklessness." The boom spreads throughout the economy.

At some point, rising demand for resources, including labor, will begin to drive up production costs [Ibid. 201]. Higher costs reduce expected future profit. That means that the value of capital as measured by the now inflated stock prices is considerably higher than the value of capital as measured by its expected future earn-ing capacity. In modern parlance, the price-to-(expected) earnings ratio is too high. The discrepancy is generally resolved in favor of expected earning capacity, so stock prices fall. Lower stock prices (and therefore capital values) means that the value of the collateral on which many loans were based shrinks. Unfortunately, the value of the debt does not shrink. Some borrowers may now be insolvent. Loans come due or are called in and new credit is not forthcoming. Liquidation may ensue; new investment will cease [Ibid. 200-1]. The downturn is magnified if the credit system is highly leveraged.

The psychological effect of the collapse of capital values makes a bad situation worse. Businessmen who once over-anticipated future earnings are now likely to adopt an overly pessimistic view of future earnings. It is difficult to be optimistic about business when bankruptcies abound and capital values have shrunk. The pessimism about future earnings translates into a decline in orders for supplies and equipment. Just as the initial increase in demand for supplies and equipment spread the prosperity to other parts of the economy, the decline in demand for supplies and equipment spreads the depression. Firms across the economy see their earnings decline, and also order fewer supplies and equipment. As Veblen wrote, "depression is primarily a malady of the affections of the business men" [Ibid. 241].

An obvious point must be emphasized: the ability of the industrial system to produce is not affected by the decline in demand or the decline in the value of capital. Over the course of the business cycle, demand and capital values rise and fall but that does not affect the underlying technological reality. A particular factory is as productive at the end of the cycle as at the beginning. In modern times the cause of economic hardship is the unwillingness of business to allow industry to operate. The fear of losing money causes businessmen to restrict both employment and the use of the tangible assets that are required to make use of the society's technology. As Veblen wrote,

> Since industry waits upon business, it is a matter of course that industrial depression is primarily a depression in business. ... Depression and industrial stagnation follow only in case the pecuniary exigencies of the situation are of such a character as to affect the traffic of the business community in an inhibitory way. But business is the quest of profits, and an inhibition of this quest must touch the seat of its vital motives. Industrial depression means that the business men engaged do not see their way to derive a satisfactory gain from letting the industrial process go forward on the lines and in the volume for which the material equipment of industry is designed. It is not worth their while, and it might even work them pecuniary harm [Ibid. 213-4].

In the end, the habits of thought of businessmen and the institution of ownership force a decline in production. The community is denied access to the equipment it needs to use its technology. A few may grumble, but most people accept the situation as normal. Habits of thought are deeply ingrained; no "right-thinking" person can expect business to operate at a loss. In fact, the legal institutions make it impossible for a business to operate at a loss for very long. Once a firm is unable to pay its bills, suppliers will not supply it and creditors will foreclose. The power of institutions is such that a kindly (or crazy) businessman cannot long operate contrary to the logic of the business system.

The behavior of business in a depression is perhaps the most obvious example of how the interests of business diverge from the interests of the community at large, but it is not the only example. There are other ways in which the logic of business causes resources to be used contrary to the best interest of the community. One such example is the practice of marketing.

The objective of business is profit. Profit is ultimately realized in the sale of goods and services. Selling is as important as producing. To use Veblen's terms, "vendibility" of output is therefore more important than "serviceability for the needs of mankind" [Ibid. 51]. Businessmen increase the vendibility of their products by devoting resources to marketing.

One form of marketing is advertising. Advertising provides a service to the community to the extent that it provides valuable information [Ibid. 57]. But most advertising is what Veblen called competitive advertising. Its purpose is "to divert purchases ... from one channel to another channel in the same general class" [Ibid. 57]. The aim of such "organized fabrication of popular convictions" [Ibid. 56-7] is to create market power. Market power allows a firm to increase its profits by raising its price and cutting its output. Obviously, it runs counter to the interest of the community as a whole. If one firm advertises, the other firms in the industry must also advertise to avoid losing market share and market power. The net effect is to raise the cost of doing business without improving the welfare of the society. Resources that could have been used to produce useful goods and services are effectively wasted.[10] Industrial output is less than what it might have been because resources devoted to it are less than what they might have been. Marketing in all its forms is one of the "parasitic lines of business" [Ibid. 64].

In Veblen's eyes, salesmanship is little more than legalized fraud. To give just one illustration, he argued that the success of the health and beauty industry depended on its ability to convince people that its products could work miracles. The chemical composition of the health and beauty aids was not as important as the faith people had in the claims made by the sellers. As Veblen put it,

> In these intimate matters of health and fabricated beauty the beneficent workings of faith are manifest; if it should not rather be said that the manifest benefit derived from these many remedies, medicaments, lotions, unguents, pastes and pigments, is in the main a work of faith which acts tropismatically on the consumer's bodily frame, with little reference to the pharmaceutical composition of the contents of the purchased container, provided that they are not unduly deleterious. The case may, not without profit, be assimilated to certain of the more amiable prodigies wrought in the name of Holy Church, where it is well known that the curative efficacy of any given sainted object is something quite apart from its chemical constitution. Indeed, here as at many other points salesmanship touches the frontiers of the magical art; and no man will question that, as a business proposition, a magical efficacy is a good thing to sell [1923, 301n].

As the marketing cliche has it, one sells "the sizzle, not the steak." The physical properties of a good are not as important as its psychological effect.

The distinction between pecuniary occupations such as marketing and industrial occupations permeates Veblen's work. Marc Tool [1977, 827] distilled the following list of contrasting examples from Veblen's writing to illustrate the pervasive nature of the distinction in Veblen's analysis:

salesmanship	workmanship
business	industry
ceremonial	technological
ownership	production
free income	tangible performance
vested interests	common man
sabotage	community serviceability
pecuniary employment	industrial employment
invidious emulation	technological efficiency
conscientious withdrawl	inordinately productive
of efficiency	enterprise
competitive advertising	valuable information & guidance
business prosperity	industrial efficiency

The terms in the right-hand column represent things that promote the well being of the community as a whole. They are, in a sense, manifestations of group-regarding instincts. Terms in the left-hand column represent things that may benefit individuals, but often at the expense of the community. They are manifestations of self-regarding instincts. A good engineer exhibits workmanship, industrial employment and community serviceability. A good banker exhibits salesmanship, pecuniary employment and sabotage. For example, a banker is much more interested in a client's sales revenue and profits than he is in the usefulness of the product. A cigarette company may be profitable, and so win a banker's favor, even though its product may be killing people. From the standpoint of banking, making money is what matters. The more general point is that making socially useful goods and making money are not the same thing.

Tariffs, quotas and other restraints on trade illustrate another way in which business interests and community interests diverge. Adam Smith observed that businessmen seek to protect themselves from competition, and that laws proposed by businessmen "ought always be listened to with great precaution, and ought never to be adopted till after having been long and carefully examined, not only with the most scrupulous, but with the most suspicious attention" [1776, 267]. Nevertheless, businessmen have deftly exploited the institution of nationalism to get laws passed to hinder foreign competitors. In so doing they have given themselves higher profits at the expense of the nation and mankind as a whole.

Veblen argued that industry (as opposed to business) is best served by a free flow of knowledge and of resources. National boundaries inhibit that flow, and the problem is made worse by imposing additional trade barriers. Even a century ago, modern science and technology were international in scope. Veblen wrote that "modern culture is drawn on too large a scale, is of too complex and multiform a character, requires the cooperation of too many and various lines of inquiry, experience and insight, to admit of its being confined within national frontiers, except at the cost of insufferable crippling and retardation" [1917, 39]. National boundaries and barriers are archaic institutions that get in the way of the further development of science and technology. "The industrial arts...have no use for and no patience with local tinctures of culture and the obstructive routine of statecraft" [1923, 440]. Nationalism, and its handmaiden patriotism, are "increasingly disserviceable" [1917, 41]. Such habits of thought held over from earlier eras are at odds with the new technological reality.

Businessmen take advantage of nationalism. They invoke the good of the country to promote their own narrow interests. As Veblen put it, "the national frontiers are a means of capitalistic sabotage" [1934, 387]. Industrial efficiency, which benefits humanity as a whole, is sacrificed on the altar of short-run profit for domestic firms. All of the tariffs, subsidies and administrative barriers "are taken for the benefit of business, to stabilise, fortify and enhance the gains of one and another among the special business Interests that are domiciled in the country" [1923, 440-1].

The point is that the community at large is best served by the efficient functioning of industry and by the free flow of knowledge, but businesses often benefit from sabotage. Business, under the guise of nationalism, get laws passed that "protect" domestic industry. By hindering foreign competitors, businesses will make more money but at the cost of "a lowered efficiency of industry on both sides of the frontier" [Veblen, 1934, 387]. The rest of the population goes along with the trade barriers because of its misplaced patriotism. A protective tariff is "a patent imbecility" [1917, 68] but such tariffs and other barriers exist due to an unholy alliance of business interest, patriotism and ignorance. The nation that imposes barriers is made worse off, as is the rest of the world.

Tariffs and similar barriers to trade are only one way in which business persuades the state to help it in its competition with businesses from other countries. A century ago Veblen noted that "business competition has become international, covering the range of what is called the world market" [1904, 293]. Business interests in each country "swing the forces of the state, legislative, diplomatic, and military, against one another in the strategic game of pecuniary advantage" [Ibid. 293]. Domestic businesses want to secure overseas resources and markets. Their control over such assets may be contested by foreign business interests or by the local citizens who resent the presence of outside interests. In such circumstances, diplomatic and military power can spell the difference between business success and failure. Businesses therefore enlist the state to help them achieve their business objectives.

Ordinary citizens, imbued with nationalistic and patriotic habits of thought, are often willing to support overseas business interests with both taxes and blood. As Veblen noted,

> Representative government means, chiefly, representation of business interests. The government commonly works in the interest of business men with a fairly consistent singleness of purpose. And in its solicitude for the business men's interests it is borne out by current public sentiment, for there is a naive, unquestioning persuasion abroad among the body of the people to the effect that, in some occult way, the material interests of the populace coincide with the pecuniary interests of those business men who live within the scope of the same set of governmental contrivances. [Ibid. 286].

The cost of the requisite military forces and of the "foreign aid" used to buy influence is paid by the nation as a whole. Yet to the extent that the nation is successful in securing advantages for its businesses, the profits accrue to business. As a result, even if the costs to the nation exceed the benefits to business, business has an incentive to enlist the state's help because it bears only a small fraction of the costs. The ordinary citizen goes along with it because he feels "that he has some sort of metaphysical share in the gains which accrue to business men who are citizens of the same 'commonwealth'" [Ibid. 289].

Yet another example of how the interests of business do not coincide with the interests of the community is provided by the "class of pecuniary experts" [1904, 29] with no permanent ties to any particular industry. The efforts of these "captains of industry" are "directed to a temporary control of the properties in order to close out at an advance" [Ibid. 31]. In other words, their objective is to buy a firm, make some changes, and then sell it at a profit. Monetary gain is all that matters; any effect on industrial output is purely incidental. As Veblen wryly observed, their "captaincy is a pecuniary rather than an industrial captaincy" [1899, 230]. It might therefore be more accurate to call them "captains of solvency" [1923, 114].

One way a captain of industry might turn a quick profit is by buying more than one firm and consolidating operations. The value of the consolidated firm may be increased for three reasons. The first is obvious; the consolidated firm will have more market power than any of the firms it absorbs. That will allow profits to increase. The second is that a larger firm may be able to take advantage of economies of scale. Veblen notes that from an industrial standpoint, the consolidation should take place as soon as the state of the industrial arts advances to a point where a larger operation would be more efficient. But business "retards the advance of industry" [1904, 45] because the consolidation is delayed while businessmen maneuver and deal. The welfare of the community would be best served by allowing industry to follow its own logic, but businessmen are only concerned about profit and loss.

The third source of gain from consolidation is the elimination of numerous non-industrial jobs. As long as there are many independent firms, each will employ its own managers, marketers, accountants and finance experts. Consolidation may make many of these jobs redundant, and so reduce costs. In his inimitable style, Veblen wrote that

> the heroic role of the captain of industry is that of a deliverer from an excess of business management. It is a casting out of business men by the chief of business men [Ibid. 48-9].

In this case, business logic may free up resources for the community. But it must be remembered that the new, larger firm will still employ people in management, marketing and the other pecuniary employments who do not act in the community's interests.

One of Veblen's best known observations about modern business is that the owners of a firm and the managers of a firm are usually not the same people. The owners of a modern corporation are its stockholders. They are absentee owners, and do not run the business. According to Veblen, "absentee ownership has become the master institution in American civilisation" [1923, 119]. As a result, managers hired by the board of directors are the ones who actually run corporations. The problem is that the interests of the managers do not coincide with the interests of the owners, let alone the interests of the community at large. Veblen observed that

> The community's interest demands that there should be a favorable difference between the material cost and the material serviceability of the output; the corporation's interest demands a favorable pecuniary difference between expenses and receipts, costs and

> sale price of the output; the corporation directorate's interest is that there be a discrepancy, favorable for purchase or for sale as the case may be, between the actual and the putative earning-capacity of the corporation's capital [1904, 158].

In other words, the community wants the most output possible for the lowest resource cost possible. The owners want to maximize long-run profits. But the people who run the company want to make a fast buck by manipulating short-run stock prices. For example, if managers own some of their firm's stock, they may issue pronounce-ments that make the firm's earnings prospects look good. That will drive up the firm's stock price. After the price has risen, the manag-ers may sell their shares. Veblen's observation sounds like today's headline. Remember Enron? The recent series of corporate scandals are merely the most egregious cases of a longstanding practice.

Managers run firms for their own benefit, and stock price ma-nipulation is not the only way managers reward themselves. Salaries of top managers are obscene and bear no relationship to their contri-bution to the firm. Executive compensation in 2004 was 431 times that of the average production worker, up from 42 times in 1982 [Economist, 2005c, 75]. Needless to say, owners are not making ten times the profit they did in 1982, and the public is not getting products that are ten times as good. Even conservative icon William F. Buckley Jr. has written about "the catastrophic conduct of some capitalist enterprises, which reward failed CEOs with hundreds of millions while playing loosely with [pension] obligations to lesser employees" [2005, 58]. How can a firm pay a poor-performing CEO hundreds of millions of dollars at the same time it is "forced" to cut pension benefits promised to other employees? Cutting pension benefits might be in the interest of the firm's owners, but the generous pay-out to a bad CEO can not be. But the owners don't make the decision; managers do. The interests of managers are distinct from everybody else's. Their predatory instinct too often swamps their group-regarding instincts.[11]

One sometimes wonders how anyone could be so greedy. If someone is already "rich," why would he suppress his better instincts for the sake of getting even more money? Isn't money supposed to have diminishing marginal utility? What could he possibly want that he doesn't already have? Veblen's answer is status. Monetary wealth is akin to a trophy in modern society. Veblen wrote that

> it is necessary, in order to ensure his own peace of mind, that an individual should possess as large a portion of goods as others with whom he is accustomed to class himself; and it is extremely gratifying to possess something more than others [1899, 31].

CEOs class themselves with other CEOs. While you and I may think that they have more than enough money, they are concerned about how they rank compared to each other.

The pursuit of status in a modern, pecuniary culture influences behavior in surprising ways. That is the topic of Veblen's most famous book, *The Theory of the Leisure Class* [1899], and is examined in the next chapters.

PART IV
CONSUMER BEHAVIOR

The economic problem begins with the fact that resources are scarce. Resources are said to be scarce because there are not enough of them to give everybody everything they want. But why do people want so much? What if you could go back in time 200 years? How would people respond if you told them that they could have indoor plumbing, electric lights, central heating and air-conditioning, power tools, automobiles, antibiotics, refrigerators, dishwashers, washing machines, radios, televisions, computers, telephones and other modern conveniences (and explained what those things were)? Most likely they would say that if they had all those things they would be in paradise, and could not imagine that they would want anything else. Today, most people in the industrialized world have all those things, but they still want more. Is there any level of economic development that will satisfy people's wants?

Veblen answered the question with an emphatic "no." Some consumption is certainly driven by the desire to meet basic needs and to make life easier, but a large portion of it is driven by the desire to gain or to maintain status. Much of what we buy is for the purpose of meeting others' expectations and to "keep up with the Joneses." In 1915 Veblen guessed that more than half of consumption expenditures were for items that were only "conventionally necessary" [1915, 272]. In other words, the expenditures were made not for physical necessity or comfort, but out of a desire to meet social expectations. Today the figure is certainly much higher. In his view, there is no level of per capita GDP that can satisfy all of our wants because the point is not just to have things, but to have more than everybody else. He wrote:

> In the nature of the case, the desire for wealth can scarcely be satiated in any individual instance, and evidently satiation of the average or general desire for wealth is out of the question. However widely, or equally, or "fairly," it may be distributed, no general increase of the community's wealth can make any approach to satiating this need, the ground of which is the desire of every one to excel every one else in the accumulation of goods. If, as is sometimes assumed, the incentive to accumulation were the want of subsistence or physical comfort, then the aggregate economic wants of a community might conceivably be satisfied at some point in the advance of industrial efficiency; but since the struggle is substantially a race for reputability on the basis of an invidious comparison, no approach to a definitive attainment is possible [1899, 32].

What is the origin of this unwinnable race? Why are we driven to run faster and faster on this treadmill?

Recall that Veblen believed that "with the exception of the instinct for self-preservation, the propensity for emulation is probably the strongest and most alert and persistent of the economic motives proper" [Ibid. 110]. People are driven to emulate others, especially those believed to be of higher status. The form of emulation and the definition of "higher" status are determined by institutions.

In the predatory barbarian era property rights emerged as claims over goods and people taken in war. The greater the warrior, the more loot he possessed. The ownership of property came to be associated with battlefield prowess, and so was associated with high status. Property gained through warfare was a type of trophy. Over time, property ownership by itself became a source of status, especially during the handicraft and machine eras. Wealth "becomes necessary to have any reputable standing in the community" [Ibid. 29]. It becomes a prerequisite for self-respect, and to earn the respect of others.

The level of wealth required depends on what others have. We want to have as much as our peers, and prefer to have more. If we have less than our peers,

> the normal, average individual will live in chronic dissatisfaction with his present lot; and when he has reached what may be called the normal pecuniary standard of the community, or of his class in the community, this chronic dissatisfaction will give place to a restless straining to place a wider and ever-widening pecuniary interval between himself and this average standard [Ibid. 31].

As the general wealth of the community grows, the average standard of wealth grows with it. A hundred years ago a telephone was an extravagant luxury; someone without a phone today is considered impoverished. To keep up with the average, we have to continually increase our own wealth. There is no absolute level of wealth that is "enough" for all time. Someone who is considered wealthy today will gradually slide down the scale of reputability unless she increases her wealth at the same rate as the overall community. The treadmill keeps going, and you will get knocked backwards if you do not keep running.

CHAPTER 9

CONSPICUOUS LEISURE AND CONSPICUOUS CONSUMPTION

In a small, tight-knit community, a person's relative wealth is generally common knowledge. In a large, industrial community most people are anonymous most of the time. If there were no clues, there would be no way for others to tell how much wealth one has. Someone with a lot of wealth would be treated like someone with very little wealth. The wealthy, therefore, want to demonstrate their wealth in order to get the respect and status that they "deserve." As Veblen put it, "in order to gain and hold the esteem of men it is not sufficient merely to possess wealth or power. The wealth or power must be put in evidence, for esteem is awarded only on evidence" [Ibid. 36].

Conventions arise as to the proper way to demonstrate one's wealth. One way is to engage in what Veblen calls "conspicuous leisure." Someone with a large amount of wealth does not have to work. As discussed earlier, there is a hierarchy of occupations, and at the top of the heap is large-scale ownership. The duties of large-scale ownership are generally nominal; others are hired to do the real work. That leaves lots of time for leisure. But just laying around the house (or mansion) all day does not provide evidence of one's wealth. People who do not know you do not know that you can afford to do nothing. You must provide evidence of your "non-productive consumption of time" [Ibid. 43].

There are many ways to accomplish that objective. One of them is to give evidence of "good breeding." That includes having knowledge of proper etiquette and manners, correct spelling and grammar, fashions, breeding of non-working animals, and other things that require time to learn but cannot be used to contribute to the material well-being of the society. Veblen points out that good manners began as a way to show good will. But they have evolved into something more complex, and now serve "to show that much time has been spent in acquiring them" [Ibid. 47]. The finer points of etiquette have the same function. Using the "wrong" fork at dinner has absolutely no effect on your ability to eat, but it is evidence that you have not spent time learning which fork to use. It implies that you did not have the leisure to do so. Your "degree of conformity to the latest accredited code of the punctilios" [Ibid. 51] is used to rank you in the hierarchy of status.

Hiring personal servants is another way to show that one does not have to do anything productive. A bonus is that the employer is regarded as the master, a position of dominance in keeping with predatory habits of thought. Some of the work that servants do is useful, but much of it is ceremonial. The fact that one can afford to exempt others from useful labor adds to one's status. The stronger and healthier the servant, the greater the conspicuous waste of money. Modern celebrities are often seen with a large entourage or "posse." The people in the entourage are employed to do very little more than just be seen. They provide evidence that the celebrity is wealthy and "important."

Another example of conspicuous leisure is the desire of people of European descent to get a tan. A century ago, people of European descent made every effort to avoid getting a tan. The difference is that a century ago, many people worked outdoors. A tan was evidence that one had to work. Today, most people work indoors. Having a tan is evidence that one has the leisure to get one. A reader may object that many people get tans because they look nice. But why do they look nice now, but did not a century ago? The answer is that tans are now fashionable, and they are fashionable because many of the wealthy have tans.

Most people do not consciously set out to emulate the rich and famous. Instead, they are affected "at the second remove" [Ibid. 84]. The wealthy (who Veblen calls "the leisure class") establish the fashions and standards that permeate the community. The standards determine what is proper, right and beautiful. They become habits of thought about how to live. The rest of the people simply try to live up to these standards in order to avoid violating convention. In other words, most people observe fashion trends simply to avoid the embarrassment that results from being out of fashion. Veblen put it as follows:

> The leisure class stands at the head of the social structure in point of reputability; and its manner of life and its standards of worth therefore afford the norm of reputability for the community. The observance of these standards, in some degree of approximation, becomes incumbent upon all classes lower in

> the scale. ... On pain of forfeiting their good name
> and their self-respect in case of failure, they must
> conform to the accepted code, at least in appearance
> [Ibid, 84].

We all want to "fit in." To do so we must follow the standards of taste accepted by the community. It is the leisure class that ultimately sets that standard.

Conspicuous consumption is another way that the wealthy can demonstrate to others how wealthy they are. Conspicuous leisure establishes standards regarding how we use our time. The practice of conspicuous consumption establishes standards regarding what goods we buy. It is the practice of consuming goods not because they meet physical needs or provide comfort, but because they show that one can afford to buy them.

Neoclassical economists might object that anything consumers buy is useful to them because it gives them utility. Veblen didn't disagree. He wrote that "whatever form of expenditure the consumer chooses, or whatever end he seeks in making his choice, has utility to him by virtue of his preference" [Ibid. 98]. But Veblen was interested in why people bought what they did. To say that people buy things because it gives them utility does not answer the question. Why does a particular good provide utility? Does it meet a biological need, does it provide comfort or convenience, or does it have a social function? It was Veblen's contention that much of what we buy is driven by social convention.

Conspicuous consumption is a way to display wealth. Buying only necessities cannot accomplish that objective, so money is spent on other things. The more extravagant and the less useful the goods, the better they are at demonstrating wealth. As Veblen wrote, "unproductive consumption of goods is honourable, primarily as a mark of prowess and a perquisite of human dignity; secondarily it becomes substantially honorable in itself" [Ibid. 69]. Buying things that others cannot afford gives one status.

Large houses, fancy cars, expensive jewelry and designer clothes are all objects of conspicuous consumption. Each item provides evidence that the owner can afford to be extravagant. Taking a bus will get you from one place to another, but driving a Mercedes Benz says something about your wealth and therefore your status. Arriving in a chauffeur-driven limousine is even better. You can sleep comfortably in a small apartment, but it is more gratifying to sleep in a mansion. The point is that there are typically many ways to meet basic needs such as transportation and lodging. How one meets those needs will tell others, especially strangers, about one's social position. Consumer behavior is as much about social signals as it is about meeting needs. The utility we receive from goods is to a significant extent derived from those social signals. We get more utility from a Rolex than from a Timex primarily because of the social statement a Rolex makes compared to that of a Timex.

Conspicuous leisure and conspicuous consumption are interrelated. One cannot just buy large quantities of goods; one must buy the best quality goods. To do so one has to spend time learning to discern what the best quality goods are. One must become a connoisseur. It takes time to learn what the best cigars and the best wines are, and knowledge of such things is evidence that one has the leisure to spend learning about unproductive things. In addition, it takes time to consume. Buying a yacht, for example, demonstrates not only that one can afford the yacht, but also that one has the leisure time to use it.

Hosting lavish dinners is another way to combine conspicuous leisure and conspicuous consumption. One can demonstrate both one's knowledge of high quality goods and one's ability to buy them. In a sense, others are enlisted to help conspicuously consume. One can also use the occasion to exhibit knowledge of the fine points of etiquette. If well-trained servants are employed, the effect is that much greater. Servants are costly and they prove that their employer is exempt from productive work. If they are well trained, it shows that time was spent instructing them in etiquette.

Conspicuous consumption also manifests in the way people dress. Dress is a particularly good vehicle for conspicuous consumption because "our apparel is always in evidence and affords an indication of our pecuniary standing to all observers at the first glance" [Ibid. 167]. Expensive clothing indicates a large ability to pay. It also typically indicates an exemption from productive labor. Wearing a tie, for example, is dangerous around machinery and therefore proves that one is further up the employment hierarchy than an industrial worker.

Clothing is needed, of course, to keep warm and to keep covered. Those needs could be met with only modest expenditure. But the purpose of clothing goes far beyond just covering. It has a large social component in that it indicates one's social position. The social pressure to conform to the established standards is so great that "it is by no means an uncommon occurrence, in an inclement climate, for people to go ill clad in order to appear well dressed" [Ibid. 168]. Wearing a suit and tie on a hot day has nothing to do with meeting human needs and everything to do with upholding social norms. Failing to wear sufficiently warm clothing on a cold winter's day because "it does not look right" is also evidence of the power of social conventions.

In an article on women's dress, Veblen presented three principles: expensiveness, novelty and ineptitude [1934, 74-5]. Expensiveness goes without saying. How can one demonstrate wealth by wearing cheap clothes? Novelty means that the clothes must be worn only for a short time. Wealth is demonstrated by continually buying new clothing. Only the latest fashions, or clothes so delicate that they will obviously wear out quickly, prove that one continually buys new clothes. Note that wearing the latest fashions will leave one with a closet full of clothes that are perfectly good for all purposes except demonstrating wealth. The waste in cloth and labor that such a closet represents is evidence that the purpose of clothing is not just to cover us. Ineptitude means that the clothes "must afford prima facie evidence of incapacitating the wearer for any gainful occupation" [Ibid. 75]. In other words, the clothing must make it obvious that the wearer cannot do anything productive. The implication is that she does not have to.

It is worth reemphasizing that most people do not consciously set out to wear clothing for the purpose of conspicuous consumption. Rather, they are simply trying to live up to the standards of taste established by the leisure class. A typical office worker does not wear a suit and tie in order to prove that he does not do manual labor. He does so because it is expected, even required. The question is, how did the custom originate? Why does it continue? The answer is that it reflects the behavior of the leisure class. Members of the leisure class establish the standards that the rest of us emulate to the best of our ability. We do so out of a fear of being ostracized for being out of step with social conventions and habits of thought.

Philosophers have long complained about the fact that the rich and famous are objects of admiration. Adam Smith wrote that

> This disposition to admire, and almost to worship, the rich and powerful, and to despise, or, at least, to neglect persons of poor and mean condition ... is ... the great and most universal cause of the corruption of our moral sentiments. That wealth and greatness are often regarded with the respect and admiration which are due only to wisdom and virtue; and the contempt, of which vice and folly are the only proper objects, is most unjustly bestowed upon poverty and weakness, has been the complaint of moralists of all ages. [1759, 61-2].

But despite the pleading of philosophers, the fact remains that the rich are objects of emulation. Veblen's argument is that humans are instinctively concerned about their status, so they pay close attention to the behavior of high-status individuals. The demeanor of the highest ranked people "is accepted as an intrinsic attribute of superior worth, before which the base-born commoner delights to stoop and yield" [Veblen, 1899, 53]. Given that tendency, how can the rich and famous not be objects of emulation?

In the modern age, tabloid magazines and television shows display the lifestyles of celebrities and billionaires for all to see. But it is not necessary to keep up with the lists of "What's Hot and What's Not" to be affected. The trendsetters, by definition, establish the trends. The trends spread throughout the society and soon become the new standards. A failure to keep up with the new standards is evidence of an inability to pay, which marks one as low status. With the exception of those with "aberrant temperament," everyone will do the best they can to avoid being ranked low in the social hierarchy. Veblen suggested that sometimes people will do without necessities in order to avoid unfavorable notice. He wrote that

> No class of society, not even the most abjectly poor, foregoes all customary conspicuous consumption. The last items of this category of consumption are not given up except under stress of the direst necessity. Very much of squalor and discomfort will be endured before the last trinket or the last pretence of pecuniary decency is put away [Ibid. 85].

Status is that important to human beings. One can observe the phenomenon in almost any city.

Conspicuous consumption alters how people perceive the value of goods. Instead of only looking at a good's ability to satisfy a physical need, people begin to consider the good's ability to demonstrate wealth. Expensive goods come to be valued because they are expensive. A good that is the most expensive of its type is the best choice for displaying wealth. The habit of thinking along these lines leads to what Veblen calls "pecuniary canons of taste." Expensive goods are preferred to cheaper ones because they are better at displaying pecuniary strength. "Without reflection or analysis, we feel that what is inexpensive is unworthy" [Ibid. 169].

Veblen gave the example of a hand-wrought silver spoon as compared to a machine-made aluminum spoon. From any functional standpoint, the two are equivalent (though Veblen gave an edge to the aluminum spoon). But the silver spoon is almost universally preferred. Why? The silver spoon has the advantage that it is more expensive, and therefore better able to demonstrate pecuniary strength. To the objection that the silver spoon is somehow more beautiful, Veblen responded by noting that "the superior gratification derived from the use and contemplation of costly and supposedly beautiful products is, commonly, in great measure a gratification of our sense of costliness masquerading under the name of beauty" [Ibid. 128]. In other words, pecuniary canons of taste affect our perception of beauty. If something is expensive, it must be beautiful. As Veblen observed, "the high gloss of ... a patent leather shoe has no more intrinsic beauty than a similarly high gloss on a threadbare sleeve" [Ibid. 131-2]. The gloss of the patent leather shoe is sought after, but the gloss of a threadbare sleeve is an embarrassment.

Machine-made goods in general are not as valued as hand-made goods. Typically, machine-made goods have fewer defects and irregularities than hand-made goods. From the standpoint of function, machine-made goods tend to be superior. But hand-made goods are usually more expensive, and are therefore preferred. The defects in hand-made goods give them "character" and are proof that they were not mass-produced.

Exceedingly few people can tell the difference between diamonds and cubic zirconia. Nevertheless, diamonds are greatly preferred. If a young man gave his fiancée a cubic zirconia engagement ring instead of a diamond ring, she would probably not know the difference. But if she discovered that it was not a diamond, she would likely break off the engagement. Diamonds are much more expensive, and therefore more desirable. Those who can't tell the difference would nevertheless probably say that diamonds are more beautiful.

A bald-faced example of pecuniary canons of taste appeared a few years back in an advertisement for Scotch whiskey. The ad read, "Twenty-one years in the cask, Twenty-six dollars the ounce." The implication, of course, was that whiskey that expensive must be good. It was also a direct appeal for conspicuous consumption. The friends of someone who might buy such expensive liquor probably read the same publications. If he bought the whiskey and served it to his friends, they would know how much it cost. So much the better.

The effect of pecuniary canons of taste on consumer spending is not typically so obvious. As with conspicuous consumption in general, we are affected at the second remove, almost sub-consciously. It creates a habit of thought that associates expensiveness with quality. Bells and whistles are added to goods "which add to the cost and add to the commercial value of the goods in question, but do not proportionately increase the serviceability of these articles for the material purposes which alone they are ostensibly designed to serve" [Ibid. 115-6]. Anyone who has ever purchased a new car will recognize the truth in that statement. Pecuniary canons of taste even apply to items that others will typically never see, such as underwear and kitchen utensils. The habit of thought is so ingrained that consumer goods that are purely functional, with no frills or flair, are very hard to find. We expect a minimal amount of decoration, fashionable design, or extraneous features. Plain products do not sell well.

On the other hand, the instinct of workmanship makes us dislike waste. Resources directed to no useful end make us uncomfortable. As a result, even goods whose real purpose is to display wealth will have at least the pretence of being useful. Veblen observed that "even in articles which appear at first glance to serve for pure ostentation only, it is always possible to detect the presence of some, at least ostensible, useful purpose" [Ibid. 100]. The wing that decorates the rear of many modern cars is supposed to stabilize them. In truth, most of the wings have very little effect. But how else can we justify to ourselves the extra expense than to pretend that they work?

CHAPTER 10

SOME IMPLICATIONS OF STATUS-DRIVEN CONSUMPTION

One of the real paradoxes of modern life is that industrial productivity is higher than it has ever been, but we do not seem to be working any less. If our wants and needs were determined by an absolute standard, then higher productivity would allow us to produce them with less effort. Over time we could work less and less without reducing our material standard of living.

But that is not the case. Our wants are continually increasing. Part of the reason is that technological change continually provides us with genuinely better products, such as medical care and pharmaceuticals. The major reason, however, is that what we want depends on what others have. Again, this does not typically stem from a crude desire to show off our wealth. Rather, it stems from a desire to fit in. As other people increase their consumption spending, we feel obliged to do the same. Increases in productivity are absorbed in the form of higher consumption. Every increase in productivity increases the socially expected standard of consumption. If we chose to work less, we would not be able to achieve that standard. What self-respecting family could go back to living as families did in 1950? The neighbors would talk and the children would be picked on at school.

Leibenstein [1950] created a taxonomy of Veblen's ideas in an attempt to put them in the context of orthodox demand theory. He identified three effects, which he labeled the bandwagon, snob and Veblen effects. Emulation is the source of the bandwagon effect. It represents "the extent to which the demand for a commodity is *increased* due to the fact that others are also consuming the same commodity" [Leibenstein, 1950, 189, emphasis in original]. In other words, it is consumers' response to social signals about what acceptable patterns of consumption are. If others are consuming a good, then, in order to fit in, we may feel the need to consume it too. Anyone who has observed the spread of a fashion trend has seen the bandwagon effect in action. If others dress in a certain way, individuals may feel awkward if their dress is "old-fashioned." They feel pressure to conform to society's norms.

The snob effect reflects the idea that while it may be good to fit in, it is even better to be a step ahead. The snob effect represents "the extent to which the demand for a consumers' good is *decreased* owing to the fact that others are also consuming the same commodity" [Ibid. 189, emphasis in original]. In other words, if one wants to demonstrate one's superiority to the masses, one cannot consume what everyone else is consuming. When the leisure class establishes a new fashion, it isn't long before it spreads due to the bandwagon effect. In order to separate themselves from everyone else, the leisure class must adopt yet another new fashion. The bandwagon and snob effects, taken together, produce an endless treadmill of fashion cycles. Once a fashion becomes popular, it loses its "cool" factor, and trendsetters must find something new.[12]

Leibenstein equates the Veblen effect with conspicuous consumption, but it is more precise to link it directly to the phenomenon of pecuniary standards of taste. It is "the extent to which the demand for a consumers' good is increased because it bears a higher rather than a lower price" [Ibid. 189]. Higher-priced goods are better at showing off one's wealth than lower-priced goods. If the object of consumption is to demonstrate one's wealth, a higher price will make a good more desirable. If the effect is strong enough, the demand curve will have a positive slope.

Steiner and Weiss [1951] added another effect, which they labeled counter-snobbery. In their view, the very rich can afford to distinguish themselves from those just rich enough to be snobs by not conspicuously consuming. People who have recently acquired wealth need to display it in order to gain the status associated with wealth. But the very rich, who are secure in their social position, can afford to avoid vulgar displays of wealth. They can even afford to adopt the "untutored expressions from the lowest orders of society" [Steiner and Weiss, 1951, 266]. In other words, the very rich may adopt the styles of the very poor in an attempt to underscore their superiority to the newly rich. They become counter-snobs.

The danger is that everyone can afford the styles of the very poor, so if the very rich adopt them, it won't be long until the bandwagon effect spreads them throughout the society. In recent years, it has become fashionable to dress like inner-city gangsters. It is fascinating to watch well-to-do people try to look like the poor and oppressed. Counter-snobbery has itself become fashionable.

Another modern paradox is that even though real incomes are at an historic high, the saving rate is at an historic low. Measurement problems might explain part of it, but there is no doubt that the savings rate is low. It would seem that as our real income rose we could afford to set aside a larger portion of it. Keynes [1964] certainly expected savings as a fraction of income to rise as income increased. That would occur if consumption were strictly for necessities and conveniences. But Veblen's point is that consumption spending has a large social component. We want to keep up with the Joneses, so as they increase their spending, we must do the same.

In the past, our local community determined our consumption standard. The goal was to consume just a little more than our neighbors did. Our local community still has a powerful influence on us, but the mass media have expanded our reference group. Even if we consume more than our neighbors do, we feel inadequate if we fall below what we think is the national standard for people like us. In addition, the mass media has exposed us to more goods and services than just those customarily consumed in our community. Exposure to goods that we didn't know existed tends to stimulate consumption spending. James Duesenberry called the phenomenon the "demonstration effect" [1967, 27].[13] Exposure to a new good may cause one to want it. We might be content at one moment, but then find ourselves longing for a good we just discovered. The overall effect is to increase consumption spending and to depress saving.

The macroeconomic effects of a low saving rate are well known and beyond the scope of this book.[14] The interested reader can find them in any macroeconomics textbook. But consider another effect. If people do not save, then they will have a difficult time supporting themselves in retirement or in times of financial crisis. That, in turn, increases popular pressure on government to "do something" about it. Higher taxes to pay for government benefits are resisted because they reduce current consumption spending. So the government borrows to pay for the benefits, which further reduces national savings.[15]

But government benefits are rarely sufficient to maintain the material standard of living one has grown accustomed to. A spell of unemployment, for example, means that even if one receives unemployment insurance, one will have to reduce consumption expenditures. That is psychologically difficult in that it means that one will not be able to spend the amount required to maintain one's social status. It is also difficult because things that were once luxuries quickly become necessities. As Veblen wrote,

> It is much more difficult to recede from a scale of expenditure once adopted than it is to extend the accustomed scale in response to an accession of wealth. Many items of customary expenditure prove on analysis to be almost purely wasteful, and they are therefore honorific only, but after they have once been incorporated into the scale of decent consumption, and so become an integral part of one's scheme of life, it is quite as hard to give up these things as it is to give up many items that conduce directly to one's physical comfort, or even that may be necessary to life and health [1899, 102-3].

There is a kind of ratchet effect. We can easily increase our consumption spending, but we have a hard time cutting it.

Even people who are employed fear unemployment because their saving is inadequate to sustain their standard of living. There is an almost constant anxiety about losing one's job because there is so little on which to fall back. Most people want to save more so as to allay such fears, but they find it very hard to do so because of the pressures to consume. Status-driven consumption makes saving difficult and then penalizes people who don't save.

The habit of thought that associates status with consumption spending is exploited and reinforced by advertising. Sometimes advertisers make a direct appeal to status: "be the first on your block to own ... ." The slogan for a recent advertising campaign in Mumbai, India was even more direct: "Owner's Pride, Neighbor's Envy" [Mehta, 2004, 35]. But most advertising is a bit more subtle. Advertising creates an image of what "normal" people are expected to consume. The implicit message is that one's neighbors are already consuming the good in question, or will be soon. The intent is to create fear of falling behind in the incessant race for reputability based on the ability to display wealth. Consumers must be kept in a constant state of unease about their social position. The ordinary pressures of watching what others in our community buy are not enough; advertisers want us to worry about what people we will never meet buy.

To that end, advertisers take full advantage of the demonstration effect. Advertisements show us goods that nobody in our community even knew existed. Without advertising we might live in blissful ignorance. But once we are aware that something exists, we may want it, or even convince ourselves that we need it. We will not be content until we buy one. And in our heart of hearts, we know that we will not be content for very long even if we do buy one.

Status-driven consumption may have one positive effect. One of the most serious concerns of the classical economists was overpopulation. They were afraid that there was a limit to how many people the available land could feed. Overpopulation is also a concern of many people in the modern world, for similar reasons. Veblen was convinced that population growth would slow because social pressure makes children expensive to raise. Children will therefore reduce other forms of socially mandated spending. He wrote that "the conspicuous consumption, and the consequent increased expense, required in the reputable maintenance of a child is very considerable and acts as a powerful deterrent" [Ibid. 113]. In modern consumer societies, the birth rate has declined dramatically, just as Veblen predicted. The drive to have children is one of the most basic human drives, but it is no match for the power of status-driven consumption.

PART V
CONCLUSION

Relatively few practicing economists are familiar with Veblen's ideas. One reason is that Veblen's own writings are so difficult to read, and the secondary literature is written mostly for specialists. But the main reason is that most economists are trained in the neoclassical tradition, and think in neoclassical terms. Equilibrium analysis, taken from Newtonian physics, dominates how economists think about the world. Veblen's Darwinian approach is alien to them. One might think that a Darwinian approach should appeal to anyone wanting to explain the continuous, cumulative change that characterizes modern economies. But as is true of other people, the habits of thought of economists are deeply ingrained. It is difficult for them to think in other than neoclassical terms. It is easier to ignore Veblen than to try to understand him.

The most pressing problem facing economists is the plight of impoverished countries. Understanding how economies evolve and change must be the first step in any useful theory of economic development.

The neoclassical approach is uniquely unsuited for such a task. An equilibrium is a position of rest. It is the opposite of change. A deep understanding of equilibrium will not help us understand change. As Easterly [2002] documents, the mainstream approach to economic development has been generally futile and enormously costly in terms of both lives and resources. We must find another way, one that recognizes the evolutionary nature of economic development.

As noted in the introduction, Veblen did not produce a complete, comprehensive theory of evolutionary economics. He was only able to develop a general approach, richly illustrated by numerous examples. But if economists had devoted their energies to developing Veblen's vision instead of pursuing the neoclassical approach, our understanding of how economies grow and change over time would certainly be much greater than it is. Time has been lost, but it is still not too late. Veblen's research program needs to be revived.

Institutions are a society's genes. They replicate themselves over time. Their relative stability insures that the society is stable over time. Each generation carries with it most of the institutions of previous generations. Nevertheless, mutations occur, primarily caused by technological change. Technological change is itself the product of our instincts of idle curiosity and of workmanship. New technologies create new opportunities and new problems, both of which can cause changes in habitual behaviors. Over long periods of time, the cumulative effect of many small changes can be revolutionary.

As the pace of technological change has increased, so has the pace of institutional change. The current era has been a time of rapid technological development, and, as Veblen predicted, it has been accompanied by rapid institutional change. Some of the changes that have occurred will endure for many years; others will die out quickly. The entire process is open-ended. There is no pre-ordained ending point, no utopia or hell to which we are inevitably being drawn. The direction of Darwinian evolution cannot be predicted. As Heraclitus put it, the only constant is change.

Veblen's call for a Darwinian method in economics is perhaps his most important contribution. But as should be clear by now, he had many other insights that are worth pursuing. Foremost among these is his argument about the central place of technology in any economy. It is a society's most important asset. Without it, we can do nothing. In fact, "resources" such as labor, machines and raw materials have economic value only because we know how to use them. Without such knowledge, they are not even resources. Economic analysis of growth must begin by recognizing the central place of technology.

Technology is a social possession, owned by the community as a whole. Individuals know bits and pieces of it, but the pieces are of little value in isolation. It is only in the context of society that the pieces gain value. What one person knows complements what others know. The more technologically advanced a community is, the more interdependent its members are. Specialists with a deep knowledge of a particular line of inquiry are possible only because there are many others to support them. The more specialized we become, the more we must depend on others. As we become increasingly specialized, we become less and less able to live without the help of countless others. We depend on the knowledge of others for virtually everything we have.

Neoclassical economists have linked the productivity of the economy to payments to the owners of labor, capital and land. In other words, property rights have been confused with productive contributions. Because there are no property rights over most of a society's technology, there is no compensation paid for its use. Compensation is paid for land, labor and capital, so economists have focused their attention on them. The essential role of technology has, until very recently,[16] been included only as an afterthought. One is reminded of the practice of adding an epicycle to Ptolemy's system every time a new observation challenged its validity. As we progress further into the "information age," Veblen's insistence that knowledge is the most important asset gains credence. Perhaps neoclassical economics will eventually go the way of Ptolemy's astronomy.

Technological change has not only transformed how and what we produce, but also how we act. New technologies have led to new patterns of behavior and have destroyed old ones. The cumulative effect of new technologies has profoundly changed our institutions and our habits of thought. Modern society, for better and for worse, is very different from earlier societies. Think about life without the automobile, the clock, the telephone or electricity. How, when, where and with whom we work and play have all been affected. Not only has our material standard of living been altered, but so have our habitual behavior and our habits of thought.

Another of Veblen's contributions is his analysis of human behavior, which is much richer than that of either neoclassical or Marxist economics. People are not one-dimensional creatures, slaves to pleasure and pain. Neither are we blank slates that are entirely the products of our environment. We are complex, sometimes contradictory beings. Veblen's approach allows for people to be people, not caricatures. Our instincts give purpose to our actions but can pull us in more than one direction. Precisely how our instincts manifest depends on the institutions we encounter; social conventions and ingrained personal habits of thought have a powerful influence over our behavior. Most of what we do is the result of habit, not rational calculation. In fact, it would be humanly impossible to rationally decide every choice we face. Over time, human behavior and attitudes evolve as institutions evolve.

The power of institutions to affect human behavior is illustrated by Veblen's explanation of consumer behavior. Consumption decisions are made for a complex set of reasons. Biological need and a desire for convenience play a role, but tradition and social expectations are of central importance. People often buy new clothes even when they have perfectly good old clothes that they never wear. The motivation is obviously not a need for warmth, but a need to meet a social objective. We are driven by our desire to emulate others, and to fit in. At the same time, our instinct of workmanship makes us dislike the waste associated with meeting society's expectations. If we reflect on our consumption decisions, we often feel internally conflicted. That just means we are human.

Perhaps the most powerful metaphor in all of economics is Adam Smith's invisible hand. According to Smith, competitive market forces channel the pursuit of self-interest into socially useful outcomes. The baker provides bread for me not because he cares about me but because he wants to make money. His motivation may be selfish, but in order to obtain his objective, he must provide me with what I want. In other words, his self-interest leads him to serve others.

Competition from other bakers forces him to maintain quality and keep prices as low as possible.

Neoclassical economics is an elaborate extension of Smith's metaphor. It posits a harmony of interests in that competitive market forces continually harness self-interest to promote social welfare. Indeed, neoclassical welfare analysis explains not only how competitive markets promote social welfare, but also cause it to be maximized.[17] Smith's idea that markets are good has been transformed into a dogma that markets are perfect.

Veblen did not dispute the fact that the rise of business institutions had, on the whole, improved the material standard of living of the average person. Even a century ago, the historical evidence was clear on this point. Today, anyone who denies that the average person in a capitalist economy would have a higher material standard of living without capitalism needs a reality check. What Veblen did deny was that capitalist institutions are perfect or harmonious. Material conditions have improved, but that does not mean that there is a harmony of interests, or that the predatory instinct is completely in check. Smith himself famously wrote that

> People of the same trade seldom meet together, even for merriment and diversion, but the conversation ends in a conspiracy against the public, or in a contrivance to raise prices. It is impossible indeed to prevent such meetings, by any law which either could be executed, or would be consistent with liberty and justice [1776, 145].

The author of the invisible hand knew that conflicts of interest existed, and that they could not be prevented. Veblen deepened our understanding of such conflicts and showed that the predatory instinct is alive and well.

An important theme in Veblen's vision is that making money is not the same thing as making useful goods. During a recession, for example, making money (or more precisely, minimizing financial losses) requires that businesses reduce output. The interest of business runs contrary to the interest of the public, who would like the output that business could produce, but doesn't. The conflict of interest is obvious. To argue that the interests of business and the interests of the public are always harmonious is to ignore reality.

Business is also more interested in the vendibility of a good than in its social usefulness. Cigarettes are profitable, so they are made and sold. The fact that they kill people is not important from a business perspective. Advertising and marketing are aimed at getting people to buy things they would not buy without it. If rational self-interest really governed human behavior, then only advertising that provided useful information would exist. As it is, enormous resources are devoted to making consumers conscious of the social image they portray by their consumption decisions. The interests of marketers and the interests of consumers do not coincide.

Smith saw a conflict between the interests of business and the interests of the public. In the corporate form of business that has come to dominate the economy, Veblen saw an additional layer of conflict. Corporations are owned by stockholders but run by professional managers. The interests of the owners still do not coincide with the interests of the public, and the interests of the managers conflict with the interests of both the public and the owners. Managers seek to enrich themselves at the expense of both the owners and the public.

As noted previously, the trend is getting worse. The management class recognizes that it can pay itself more or less anything it wants, so it does. There is no invisible hand to insure that the self-interest of CEOs is channeled into socially useful outcomes. There is not even an invisible hand to insure that CEOs don't rob the owners. CEOs control capitalism's dominant institution, and are aware of their power.

When thinking about the flaws in our economic institutions there is a natural tendency to want to "do something" about them. Veblen would occasionally hint at a remedy. He was especially enamored of the displays of workmanship exhibited by engineers and technicians, especially in contrast to the sabotage resulting from business interests. He quipped that

> The effective management of the industrial system at large is already in the hands of the technicians, so far as regards the work actually done; but it is all under the control of the Vested Interests, representing absentee owners, so far as regards its failure to work [1921, 163].

But for the most part, Veblen limited himself to analysis, not prescription. There are two main dangers associated with trying to "fix" things. The first is that, without a complete understanding of how the institutions in question relate to other institutions, one cannot be sure that the cure will be better than the disease. Remember that institutions are like a society's genes. Tinkering with them without a deep understanding can lead to unexpected consequences. The history of the twentieth century is full of the tragic consequences of well-intentioned "improvements." That is why pursuing Veblen's research program is so important; we need to understand the process much better than we do if we ever hope significantly to improve things.

The second danger is that any conscious change must be approved by the existing institutional structure. Not only will there be resistance from vested interests, but prevailing habits of thought about what is "natural" and "normal" are hard to change. The power of "imbecile institutions" to prevail, even when millions of lives are at stake (as was the case before WWI), should not be underestimated. Vested interests, combined with the inertia of prevailing habits, are hard to overcome. Significant social change requires a change in how people think. Imposing change from the top down usually requires an iron fist and bloodshed. Revolutionaries the world over have often exacted a high price for their vision of a better society, and in their ignorance they have often made things worse rather than better. Perhaps Friedrich Engels said it best when he wrote that

> People who boasted that they made a revolution have always seen the next day that they have no idea what they were doing, that the revolution made did not in the least resemble the one they would have liked to make. That is what Hegel calls the irony of history [1885, 438].

How could it turn out any other way? Veblen understood that deeply ingrained habits cannot be changed overnight. Passing new laws will not alter how people think. As a result, change will be resisted because it runs counter to what people "know" to be true and right. The greater the change, the greater the resistance and the greater the likelihood of violence. Would-be revolutionaries need to read and understand Veblen.

What is required is a revolution in economics. The profession must take up Veblen's challenge. As noted in the introduction, Veblen believed that "the question now before the body of economists is not how things stabilise themselves in a 'static state,' but how they endlessly grow and change" [1934, 8]. The question remains the same today. Economists have no real theory of growth and change. The focus is on quantitative change, as measured by increases in GDP or in the stocks of capital and labor. The evolution of the institutional structure is the key to understanding growth, but is largely ignored. At best, economists will make a list of institutions that might speed the growth of GDP, but are at a loss to explain how those institutions might come about, and how they can be made an integral part of the society's culture.

Veblen offers a starting point for those wanting to develop a real theory of growth. Some work has been done by what is known as the institutional school of thought. But what is needed is a much deeper and broader effort, on par with the effort devoted to neoclassical theory. The path will be difficult, and answers are not guaranteed. But the potential rewards are priceless.

REFERENCES

Adams, Roy D. and Ken McCormick (1992), "Fashion Dynamics and the Economic Theory of Clubs," Review of Social Economy, 50, 24-39.

Ambrose, Stanley H. (2002), "Small Things Remembered: Origins of Early Microlithic Industries in Sub-Saharan Africa," in Robert G. Elston and Steven L. Kuhn, Eds., Thinking Small: Global Perspectives on Microlithization, American Anthropological Association.

Ambrose, Stanley H. (2005), Private e-mail.

Aristotle (1984), The Complete Works of Aristotle, edited by Johnathan Barnes, Princeton University Press: Princeton.

Aspromourgos, Tony (1986), "On the Origin of the Term 'Neoclassical'," Cambridge Journal of Economics, 10, 265-70.

Brette, Olivier (2003), "Thorstein Veblen's Theory of Institutional Change: Beyond Technological Determinism," European Journal of the History of Economic Thought, 10, 455-77.

Buckley, William F. (2005), "Whose Money Is It?" National Review, June 20, 58.

Clark, John Bates (1899/1965), The Distribution of Wealth, Augustus M. Kelley: New York.

Coats, A. W. (1954), "The Influence of Veblen's Methodology," Journal of Political Economy, 62, 529-37.

Cox, W. Michael and Koo, Jahyeong (2006) "Miracle to Malaise: What's Next for Japan? Economic Letter, Vol. 1, No. 1, Federal Reserve Bank of Dallas.

Diggins, John P. (1977), "Animism and the Origins of Alienation: The Anthropological Perspective of Thorstein Veblen," History and Theory, 16, 113-26.

Diggins, John P. (1999), Thorstein Veblen, Theorist of the Leisure Class, Princeton University Press: Princeton.

"Dilbert," (2005) Waterloo Courier, June 30, C9.

Dorfman, Joseph (1934/1972), Thorstein Veblen and His America, Augustus M. Kelley: Clifton NJ.

Duesenberry, James (1967), Income, Saving, and the Theory of Consumer Behavior, Oxford University Press: New York.

Easterly, William (2002) The Elusive Quest for Growth, The MIT Press: Cambridge.

The Economist (2004a), "Another Health Disaster," June 23.

The Economist (2004b), "A Brother for Her," December 16.

The Economist (2005a), "An Unexpectedly Bright Idea," Technology Supplement, June 11.

The Economist (2005b), "The CrackBerry Backlash," June 25.

The Economist (2005c), "Too Many Turkeys," November 26.

The Economist (2006), "A Survey of Germany," February 11.

Edgell, Stephen (2001), Veblen in Perspective: His Life and Thought, M.E. Sharpe: Armonk, NY.

Edgeworth, F.Y. (1881), Mathematical Psychics, C. Kegan Paul & Co.: London.

Engels, Friedrich (1885/1975), "A Letter to Zasulich," in Karl Marx and Friedrich Engels: Selected Correspondance, 1846-1895, Vol. XXIX, Greenwood Press: Westport.

Fayazmanesh, Sasan (2003), "On Veblen's Coining of the Term 'Neoclassical'," in Rick Tilman (editor), The Legacy of Thorstein Veblen, Vol. I, Edward Elgar: Cheltenham, 486-509.

Friedman, Milton (1953), "The Methodology of Positive Economics," in Essays in Positive Economics. Chicago: University of Chicago Press.

Friedman, Milton and Friedman, Rose (1980), Free to Choose, Harcourt, Brace, Jovanavich: New York.

Goldberg, Jonah (2005), "Dan, Done," National Review, March 28, 6.

Herskovits, Melville J. (1936), "The Significance of Thorstein Veblen for Anthropology," American Anthropologist, 38 (New Series), 351-3.

Hodgson, Geoffrey M. (1992), "Thorstein Veblen and Post-Darwinian Economics, Cambridge Journal of Economics, 16, 285-301.

Hunt, E.K. (1979), History of Economics Thought, Wadsworth Publishing: Belmont, California.

Keynes, John Maynard (1964), The General Theory of Employment, Interest and Money, Harcourt, Brace & World: New York.

Jennings, Ann and Waller, William (1994), "Evolutionary Economics and Cultural Hermeneutics: Veblen, Cultural Relativism and Blind Drift," Journal of Economic Issues, 28, 997-1030.

Leibenstein, Harvey (1950), "Bandwagon, Snob and Veblen Effects in the Theory of Consumers' Demand," Quarterly Journal of Economics, 64, 183-207.

Lucas, Robert E. (1988), "On the Mechanics of Economic Development," Journal of Monetary Economics, 22, 3-42.

Mankiw, N. Gregory (2003), Macroeconomics, 5th edition, Worth Publishers: New York.

Mankiw, N. Gregory (2004), Principles of Economics, third edition, Thomson-Southwestern: Mason, OH.

Marx, Karl, (1859/1978), Preface to "A Contribution to the Critique of Political Economy" in Robert C. Tucker, The Marx-Engels Reader, New York: W.W.Norton & Company.

McCormick, Ken (1983), "Duesenberry and Veblen: The Demonstration Effect Revisited," Journal of Economic Issues, , 1125-1129.

McCormick, Ken (1986), "Towards a Definition of Waste in Economics: A Neoinstitutional Approach," Review of Social Economy, 44: 80-92.

McCormick, Ken (1988), "Important Parallels between Veblen and Keynes," Journal of Economics, 14, 116-121.

McCormick, Ken, (2002), "Veblen and the New Growth Theory: Community as the Source of Capital's Productivity," Review of Social Economy, 60: 263-77.

Mehta, Suketu (2004), Maximum City: Bombay Lost and Found, Alfred A. Knopf: New York.

Mill, John Stuart (1961), "Utilitarianism," in Max Lerner, Ed., Essential Works of John Stuart Mill, Bantam Books: New York.

Mills, C. Wright (1953), "Introduction," in Thorstein Veblen, The Theory of the Leisure Class, Mentor Books: New York.

Mokyr, Joel, (2002), The Gifts of Athena: Historical Origins of the Knowledge Economy, Princeton University Press: Princeton.

Mouhammed, Adil H. (2003), An Introduction to Thorstein Veblen's Economic Theory, The Edwin Mellen Press: Lewiston NY.

Pareto, Vilfredo (1897), "The New Theories of Economics," Journal of Political Economy, 5: 485-502.

Rutherford, Malcolm (1984), "Thorstein Veblen and the Process of Institutional Change," History of Political Economy, 16, 331-48.

Rutherford, Malcom (2001), "Institutional Economics: Then and Now," Journal of Economic Perspectives, 15, 173-194.

Smith, Adam (1759/1982), The Theory of Moral Sentiments, Liberty Classics: Indianapolis.

Smith, Adam (1776/1976), The Wealth of Nations, Liberty Classics: Indianapolis.

Smith, Adam (1795/1982), "The History of Astronomy," in Essays on Philosophical Subjects, Liberty Classics: Indianapolis.

Sowell, Thomas (1967), "The 'Evolutionary' Economics of Thorstein Veblen," Oxford Economic Papers, 19: 177-198.

Spengler, Joseph J. (1972), "Veblen on Population and Resources," Social Science Quarterly, 52: 861-78.

Steiner, Robert L. and Joseph Wiess (1951), "Veblen Revised in the Light of Counter-Snobbery," Journal of Aesthetics and Art Criticism, 9, 263-8.

Tilman, Rick (1992), Thorstein Veblen and His Critics, 1891-1963, Princeton University Press: Princeton.

Tilman, Rick (1993), A Veblen Treasury: From Leisure Class to War, Peace and Capitalism, M.E.Sharpe: Armonk, N.Y.

Tilman Rick (2003), The Legacy of Thorstein Veblen, Edward Elgar Publishing, Inc.: Northampton, MA.

Tool, Marc (1977), "A Social Value Theory in Neoinstitutional Economics," Journal of Economic Issues, 11, 823-46.

Veblen, Thorstein (1899/1965) The Theory of the Leisure Class, Augustus M. Kelley: New York.

Veblen, Thorstein (1904/1975) The Theory of Business Enterprise, Augustus M. Kelley: New York.

Veblen, Thorstein (1914/1964), The Instinct of Workmanship, Augustus M. Kelley: New York.

Veblen, Thorstein (1915/1964), Imperial Germany, Augustus M. Kelley: New York.

Veblen, Thorstein (1917/1964), An Inquiry into the Nature of Peace, Augustus M. Kelley: New York.

Veblen, Thorstein (1918/1965), The Higher Learning in America, Augustus M. Kelley: New York.

Veblen, Thorstein (1919/1990) The Place of Science in Modern Civilization. New Brunswick and London: Transaction Publishers.

Veblen, Thorstein [1921/1965], The Engineers and the Price System, Augustus M. Kelley: New York.

Veblen, Thorstein [1923/1964], Absentee Ownership, Augustus M. Kelley: New York.

Veblen, Thorstein [1934/1964], Essays in Our Changing Order, Augustus M. Kelley: New York.

Walker, Donald A. (1977), "Thorstein Veblen's Economic System," Economic Inquiry, XV, 213-237.

FOOTNOTES

[1] Those wanting to learn more about Veblen after reading this book may want to see Tilman's [2003] 3-volume collection of articles about Veblen, or his [1993] edited volume of Veblen's own writing.

[2] Neoclassical economics is the label that Veblen gave to the economic orthodoxy of his time, which had its roots in classical economics. The label stuck, and is widely used to this day. See Aspromourgos [1986], Fayazmanesh [2003] and Veblen [1919, 175].

[3] See the essays by Hodder, Tilman and Stabile reprinted in Tilman, 2003, vol. III.

[4] There is a strain of the "new institutional economics" that argues that institutions evolve toward efficient forms. Veblen would have rejected that viewpoint in the strongest possible terms. See Rutherford, 2001, 187.

[5] Friedman and Friedman [1980, 11-13] used the same example to illustrate the power of markets.

[6] See, for example, Mankiw, 2004, 405.

[7] Keynes reached the same conclusion from a different premise. See Keynes [1964] 213.

[8] At the time Veblen was writing, running a business was an overwhelmingly male occupation.

[9] Note the similarity to Keynes. See McCormick, 1988.

[10] See McCormick, 1986

[11] A recent comic strip makes fun of the practice. It reads, "The board has learned that you've been dipping employees in varnish and using them as office furniture. We voted to fire you. Your severance package includes $100 million, the corporate jet, perpetual benefits and a salary of $1 million per year" [Dilbert, 2005].

[12] For another approach to these issues, see Adams and McCormick [1992].

[13] For Duesneberry's relationship to Veblen, see McCormick, 1983.

[14] In brief, low savings leads either to less investment or to a dependence on foreign capital.

[15] National saving is private saving plus public saving. Government borrowing makes public saving negative.

[16] For a discussion of Veblen and the "new" neoclassical growth theory, see Mc-Cormick, 2002.

[17] See, for example, Mankiw, 2004, 137-154.

INDEX

Printed in the United States
66216LVS00005B/334-357